Poptropica® English Islands

TEST BOOKLET 6

P **Pearson**

Contents

Introduction	3
Preparation for evaluation	4
Placement	5
Unit 1	8
Unit 2	12
Unit 3	16
Unit 4	20
Unit 5	24
Unit 6	28
Unit 7	32
Unit 8	36
End of term 1	40
End of term 2	44
End of term 3	48
Final	52
Exam preparation	60
Answer Key	72
Audioscript	78
Evaluation chart	85

Evaluation can be described as an attempt to analyse the learning that a pupil has achieved over a period of time as a result of the classroom teaching/learning situation. It plays an integral part in the teaching and learning process.

The evaluation material in this Test Booklet has been designed to analyse pupils' progress, with the aim of reinforcing the positive aspects and identifying areas for improvement.

There are five main reasons for evaluation:

Formative – to increase motivation by making evaluation a part of the continuous learning process.

Summative – to give pupils feedback on their progress or achievement at a particular point in time, often formally through tests.

Informative – to give pupils and parents feedback on progress or achievements.

Diagnostic – to monitor individual pupils' needs and help identify pupils who need special support.

Evaluative – to identify pupils' level of achievement and select or order pupils according to merit, to check effectiveness of teaching methods, teaching materials and teachers.

This Test Booklet contains one Placement test, eight Unit tests, three End of term tests, one Final test, and one Exam preparation test.

The Placement test can be used as a diagnostic test at the start of the year, reviewing learning from the previous year and helping to assess pupils' ability.

The Unit tests can be used at the end of each unit, to monitor pupils' progress through the course, to give pupils feedback on their achievement and to identify areas requiring reinforcement.

The End of term and Final tests can be used as informative and evaluative tests, for reporting purposes.

The Exam preparation test can be used to help prepare pupils for external exams such as CYLETS and Trinity.

A and B versions have been provided for the Unit tests, the Final test and the Exam preparation test. Both versions cover exactly the same learning objectives, and will provide an equal level of evaluation. You may find it useful to hand out different A and B versions to students who sit next to each other. Alternatively, you could use the A version to test the whole class and use the B version for reinforcement purposes.

The four skills of Reading, Writing, Listening and Speaking are tested through self-explanatory activities that students will be familiar with from their work in class.

Each activity has its own score, with a consolidated score at the end of each page and a total score at the end of each test. Points have been allocated according to the number of tasks pupils are required to do in each activity.

For Speaking activities, points have been allocated according to the learning objectives. In the lower levels of the course, points should be awarded for correct word identification. In the higher levels of the course, longer answers are expected, and points should be awarded for production of the target language. Pupils should be allowed to make more than one attempt, and you should encourage them to self-correct.

Procedure on the day before the evaluation

- Review unit content using games to give practice for the coming evaluation.
- Ask pupils to predict what they think the content of the evaluation might be, using L1 as needed.

Procedure on the day of evaluation

- Play a game and sing a song or chant to help pupils to move from L1 to English.
- Play the audio and direct pupils to complete the listening activities. Audio files are available on the Active Teach, or at pearsonelt.com/catalogue/primary/poptropica-english-islands.
- As with the audio throughout this course, you may wish to pause the audio to allow pupils to complete each question.
- Depending on your classroom setup, you may wish to set pupils up in pairs to complete the speaking activity and monitor the class as a whole. Alternatively, you may prefer to have pupils speak individually to you while the remainder of the class works through the reading and writing exercises.
- Have some small pieces of scrap paper available for students to make notes for their speaking evaluation. Emphasise that they only should make notes. Try to avoid full sentences or scripts being written.
- Set pupils a time limit within which to complete the remainder of the test.
- Pupils will need colouring pens or pencils for some of the activities.
- Check the answers against the Answer Key on pages 72–77. Please note that the answers for the speaking activities are intended as suggested answers only. Write the total score in the space provided at the bottom of each page and at the end of the tests.
- When handing tests back to pupils, go through the answers and explain any errors.

Poptropica English Islands also encourages the practice of self-evaluation, which is provided at the end of each unit in the Activity Book. This gives the pupils an important opportunity to express their own opinion about their progress in English.

1 Read and circle. Then match. (16 points)

1 What (was / were) you doing yesterday at 6 pm?
2 Whose books are (this / these)?
3 How (much / many) are those trousers?
4 What (are / is) Jane like?
5 (When / Where) did you go to Paris?
6 (Was / Were) the film interesting?
7 Is she (taller / tallest) than him?
8 Did you have English (on / in) Tuesday?

a No, he's the tallest.
b I was studying Maths.
c Yes, I did.
d No, it wasn't. It was boring.
e They are £20. They are not too expensive!
f She's very friendly and talkative.
g They're hers.
h I went on August 1st.

2 Read. Then match. (6 points)

1 You do this to pass a test.
2 He's talkative.
3 A musical instrument.
4 You have one of these with candles on your birthday.
5 This person plans and designs bridges.
6 You wear this with jeans, trousers or skirts.

3 Read. Then write T = True or F = False. (6 points)

Hi. I'm Rowena. I'm eleven. I live in a small town near the sea. My school is in the middle of the town. I walk to school every day. I like walking. It's ten minutes from my house to school. I go past the library and the bookshop and walk towards the river. There's a bridge across the river. My school is across the bridge and behind the swimming pool. At the weekends, I go to the beach with my family. In summer, we go camping. I love camping. Sometimes we stay on the campsite all day. Sometimes we go on day trips. We visit castles, museums and parks. My favourite trip is to the National Park near the campsite.

There is a big lake in the middle of the park and you can see lots of beautiful birds. I love watching the ducks. In the evening, we sometimes watch otters swimming in the lake. Last year, we saw an otter and her family. We watched the baby otters play in the water for two hours. It was dark when we went back to the campsite.

1 Rowena lives near the sea. ☐
2 Rowena goes across a river to get to school. ☐
3 In summer, they go to the beach. ☐
4 The campsite is in the National Park. ☐
5 There are ducks in the National Park. ☐
6 The baby otters played for two hours. ☐

Score: ___ /28

1 **Write the questions. (6 points)**

1 _____ He's very clever but a bit shy.

2 _____ She's good at writing stories.

3 _____ I went to the beach yesterday.

4 _____ I'm going to buy some sunglasses.

5 _____ I was watching TV yesterday evening.

6 _____ I go running twice a week.

2 **Put the words in order to make sentences. (5 points)**

1 good / sports / Ellie / is / at

   _____.

2 playground / in / was / the / ball / the

   _____.

3 with / tennis / friends / played / my / I

   _____.

4 dog / I / walking / was / yesterday / the

   _____.

5 which / very / is / American / film / an / it's / famous

   _____.

3 **My free time. What did you do yesterday after school? Write. (9 points)**

- Did you go shopping/to the cinema?
- Yesterday I was playing video games/reading/rollerblading …
- Were you with your friends?

_____

_____

_____

_____

_____

Score: ____ /20

1 02 **Listen. Then complete. (11 points)**

birds	boat	Brazil	camping	hiking	next week
quickly	saw	tomorrow	uncle	very	

This is Andy. He's my ¹_____. He's a tour guide. He goes to a lot of different countries. ²_____ he is going to Colombia and ³_____, he is going to China. Sometimes he takes groups ⁴_____. He likes camping. He can pitch a tent very ⁵_____ and he can pitch it in the dark! Sometimes he takes a group ⁶_____ in the hills and mountains or on ⁷_____ trips in Brazil.

Last year I went with him to ⁸_____. It was great. One day we went on a boat trip on the Amazon River. It was ⁹_____ foggy on the river when we got to the boat. But it was beautiful. From the boat we could hear the sounds of ¹⁰_____ and monkeys in the trees. They were very noisy! And we ¹¹_____ some tapir drinking water from the river. It was amazing. I want to be a tour guide when I'm older!

2 03 **Listen and circle. Then listen again and match. (12 points)**

1 What were you doing yesterday at (5 o'clock / 4 o'clock), Sarah?

2 What (are / were) you doing yesterday morning before school, Ed?

3 What does (Sarah / Harry) look like?

4 (What's / What is) Harry like?

5 Do you take (notes in class / the rubbish out)?

6 (Did / Could) you go to the party last weekend?

a Yes, I do.

b No, I couldn't. My grandparents were visiting.

c I was walking home from school.

d He's sporty and hard-working.

e He's got short, blond hair and blue eyes.

f I was having my breakfast and finishing my homework for today!

3 **Look. What can you see? Answer your teacher's questions. (7 points)**

Score: ___ /30

Whole test score: ___ /78

1 **Put the letters in order to make words. Then match. (10 points)**

1 chort   _ _ _ _ _ _

2 staicemp   _ _ _ _ _ _ _ _ _

3 ntet   _ _ _ _

4 posscam   _ _ _ _ _ _ _

5 rife   _ _ _ _

a

b

c

d

e

2 **Read. Then match. (6 points)**

1 pitch   **a** a compass

2 set up   **b** a tent

3 light   **c** the rain

4 read   **d** the pegs

5 put in   **e** the beds

6 keep out of   **f** a fire

3 **Read. Then complete. (7 points)**

> camping   compass   fire   lighting   put   sleeping bags   tents

I'm at an adventure camp with my class. It's great! We're [1]_____.
Our campsite is in the forest. There are sixteen children. Some of the boys
and girls are good at pitching [2]_____. I can't pitch a tent but I can
[3]_____ in the pegs. It's evening so I'm putting the [4]_____
inside. I've got a new one. It's very warm. It's got feathers inside.
This evening, we're [5]_____ a fire. We like singing songs around
the [6]_____.
Tomorrow we start hiking in the hills at 9 am. I've got a map and
[7]_____ and I have to find the route.

4 **Think of a favourite place by the sea or river. Then write. (7 points)**

• What's it like?   • Are there any mountains/valleys/caves …?   • What do you like doing there?

_____

_____

Score: ____ /30

_____

1 Adventure camp

1 🎧 **Listen. Then write T = True or F = False. (5 points)**

1 The family are on an adventure camp. ☐

2 Will isn't good at sports. ☐

3 Joanna's mum likes camping. ☐

4 Sarah and Kim are Joanna's friends. ☐

5 Sarah and Kim are not putting in the tent pegs. ☐

2 🎧 **Listen. Then circle. (4 points)**

1 Will (can / can't) pitch a tent.

2 Joanna's mum can (pitch a tent / read a compass).

3 Sarah and Kim can't (light a fire / take down a tent).

4 Sonia hasn't got her (sleeping bag / rucksack).

3 **Look at the adventure camp. Then talk. (6 points)**

- What are the people doing?

- He's/She's ... putting/pitching/lighting/laying out ...

- He/She can/can't ...

- I love ... He/She loves ...

Score: ___ /15

Whole test score: ___ /45

1 **Read. Then write and match. (10 points)**

1 Something which helps you pitch a tent. _____

2 A large bag which you sleep in when camping. _____

3 A big bag often used by campers. _____

4 A small light which you carry in your hand. _____

5 This always shows north. _____

ⓐ ⓑ ⓒ ⓓ ⓔ

2 **Look. Then complete. (6 points)**

1 2 3 4 5 6

1 They're _____.   2 They're _____.

3 He's _____.   4 They're _____.

5 She's _____.   6 He's _____.

3 **Read. Then complete. (7 points)**

campsite   compass   setting up   lighting
putting in   pitch   tents

I'm at an adventure camp with my friends. Our ¹_____ is in the mountains next to a small river. There are four families – eight children and our mums and dads. We're pitching four ²_____. My friend, Bob, can ³_____ a tent but he can't read a compass. I'm ⁴_____ the pegs. Jane is ⁵_____ the beds. This evening, we're ⁶_____ a campfire. Tomorrow, we start rock climbing in the mountains at 1 pm. Mum's got the map and ⁷_____.

4 **Think of an adventure camp. What's it like? Then write. (7 points)**

- What's it like? • Are there any mountains/valleys/caves ...? • What do you like doing there?

_____

_____

_____

Score: ___ /30

1 **Listen. Then circle. (5 points)**

1 Joanna is camping with her (friends / family).
2 Will (is / isn't) good at sports.
3 Joanna's mum and dad (don't like / like) camping.
4 Sarah and Kim are (older / younger) than Joanna.
5 Sarah and Kim (are / aren't) putting in the pegs.

2 **Listen. Then write T = True or F = False. (4 points)**

1 Will can pitch a tent. ☐

2 Joanna's mum can't read a compass. ☐

3 Sarah and Kim can't light a fire. ☐

4 Sonia hasn't got her sleeping bag. ☐

3 **Look at the adventure camp. Then talk. (6 points)**

- What are the people doing?
- He's/She's ... putting/pitching/lighting/laying out ...
- He/She can/can't ...
- I love ... He/She loves ...

Score: ___ /15

Whole test score: ___ /45

1 **Read and look. Then match. (12 points)**

1 rh — mel
2 ch — ala
3 ko — ino
4 le — ale
5 ca — eetah
6 wh — mur

 **a**
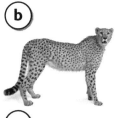 **b**
c
d
e
f

2 **Put the words in order to make questions. Then match. (8 points)**

1 heavy / how / a / rhino / is

_____?

2 a / is / tall / giraffe / how

_____?

3 dangerous / cheetahs / than / more / are / lemurs

_____?

4 longest / is / which / the

_____?

a It's five metres tall.
b The whale is the longest.
c It's 1,600 kilogrammes.
d Yes, they are.

3 **Look and write. (4 points)**

1 Which is the tallest?
_____

2 Which is the longest?
_____

3 Which is the slowest?
_____

4 Which is the lightest?
_____

4 **Write about your favourite animal. (6 points)**

• What is it?
• How big/heavy/tall … is it?

• Is it taller/shorter/heavier … than a …?
• Is it the tallest/shortest/fastest … animal?

_____

_____

_____

Score: ____ /30

1 Listen. Then number in the correct order. (8 points)

a whale ☐	b butterfly ☐	c rhino ☐	d cheetah ☐
e koala ☐	f otter ☐	g camel ☐	h lemur ☐

2 Listen and circle. Then match. (12 points)

1 Are whales (bigger / longer) than otters?
2 Which is the (tallest / heaviest), the rhino or the turtle?
3 Is the (tiger / cheetah) the lightest animal?
4 Are (seals / turtles) taller than rhinos?
5 Which is the (biggest / smallest): the otter, the koala or the lemur?
6 How (tall / fast) is the cheetah?

a No, it isn't.
b No, they aren't.
c Yes, they are.
d Very fast!
e The lemur.
f The rhino.

3 Look at the animals. Then talk. (10 points)

- What animals are …?
- Which animal is …?
- Are/Is … biggest/smallest/lightest/heaviest/longest/shortest …?
- How tall/heavy/big … is it/are they?

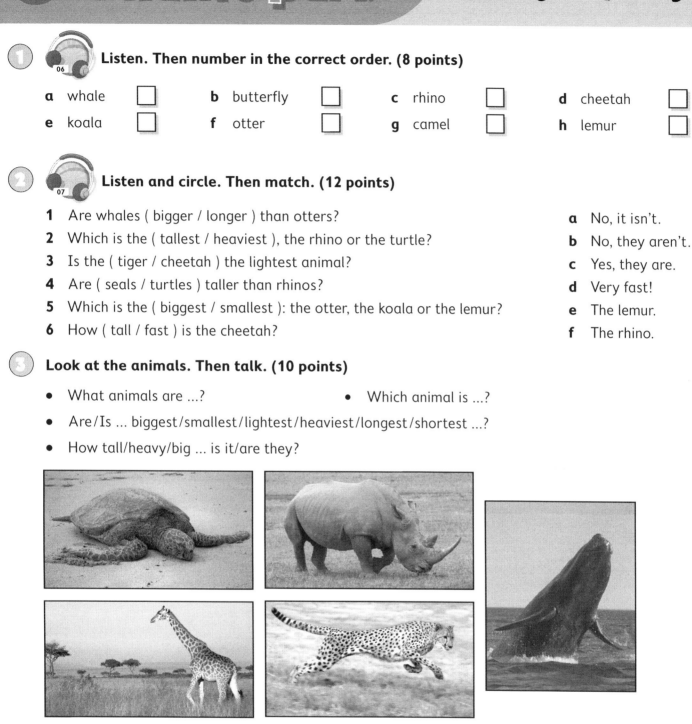

Score: ___ /30

Whole test score: ___ /60

1 **Put the letters in order to make words. Then match. (12 points)**

1 lesa _____

2 greti _____

3 retot _____

4 rultet _____

5 hiron _____

6 aolka _____

a

b

c

d

e

f

2 **Put the words in order to make questions. Then match. (8 points)**

1 an / is / long / elephant / how

_____?

2 a / heavy / how / cheetah / is

_____?

3 tigers / than / more / are / turtles / dangerous

_____?

4 heaviest / is / which / the

_____?

a Yes, they are.

b The hippo is the heaviest.

c It's three metres long.

d It's 60 kilogrammes.

3 **Look and write. (4 points)**

1 Which is the smallest?

_____

2 Which is the fastest?

_____

3 Which is the biggest?

_____

4 Which is the lightest?

_____

4 **Write about a wild animal. (6 points)**

- What is it?

- How big/heavy/tall ... is it?

- Is it taller/shorter/heavier ... than a ...?

- Is it the tallest/shortest/fastest ... animal?

_____

_____

_____

Score: ____ /30

1 🎧 06 **Listen. Then number in the correct order. (8 points)**

a otter ☐   **b** lemur ☐   **c** camel ☐   **d** rhino ☐

e butterfly ☐   **f** cheetah ☐   **g** whale ☐   **h** koala ☐

2 🎧 07 **Listen and write. Then match. (12 points)**

1 Are whales _____ than otters?

2 Which is the _____, the rhino or the turtle?

3 Is the _____ the lightest animal?

4 Are _____ taller than rhinos?

5 Which is the _____: the otter, the koala or the lemur?

6 How _____ is the cheetah?

a The rhino.

b No, it isn't.

c No, they aren't.

d The lemur.

e Very fast!

f Yes, they are.

3 **Plan a tour of a wildlife park. Then talk. (10 points)**

- What animals are the fastest / biggest …?
- Are/Is … found/rescued/seen … in …?
- Which animal is the heaviest / smallest …?

_____

_____

_____

_____

Score: ____ /30

Whole test score: ____ /60

1 **Read. Then complete. (6 points)**

end   first   in   house   station   straight

How do you get to the railway ¹_____? Start at your house and go ²_____ ahead.

At the ³_____ of the road, turn right. Go up the road ⁴_____ front of the guest

⁵_____ and walk to the end of the road. Take the ⁶_____ road on the right.

2 **Look at the map. Then read and write. (14 points)**

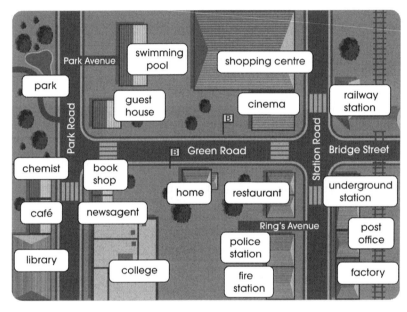

1 Start at home. Turn right out of the house and go straight ahead. Turn left into Station Road. Go straight ahead. Go past the cinema. It's the next place on the left.

It's the _____.

2 Start at the shopping centre. Come out of the shopping centre and turn right. Continue straight ahead. Turn right into Green Road. Walk to the end of the road. At the end of the road, turn right into Park Road. Take the first road on the right. It's the building at the end of the road.

It's the _____.

3 Start at home. _____

_____.

It's the newsagent.

4 Start at the college. _____

_____.

It's the police station.

Score: ___ /20

1 Listen. Then circle. (5 points)

1 The supermarket is ...
- **a** behind the library.
- **b** next to the swimming pool.
- **c** next to the post office.

2 The newsagent's is ...
- **a** on the corner.
- **b** between the bookshop and the chemist.
- **c** opposite the theatre.

3 The station is ...
- **a** over the bridge.
- **b** at the end of the high street.
- **c** in front of the cinema.

4 Al wants to go to ...
- **a** the college.
- **b** the factory.
- **c** the bus stop.

5 There isn't a ...
- **a** newsagent's.
- **b** shopping centre.
- **c** post office.

2 Listen. Then complete. (5 points)

1 If the weather is good, _____ can go to the park.

2 I can go to the _____ if I'm not too tired.

3 If you're ill, you _____ go to the chemist's.

4 If you want to have fun, we can go to the _____.

5 If you _____ your homework, you can come to the shopping centre.

3 Look at the map. Then talk. (5 points)

- Is/Are there ...?
- How do you get to the ...?
- If you ...
- It's on the corner/at the end/in front of ...

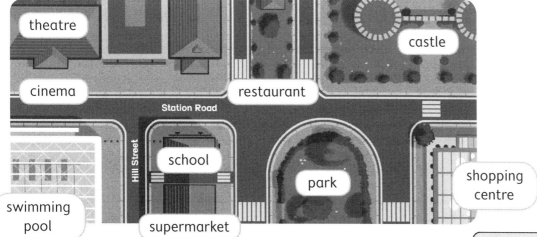

Score: ___ /15

Whole test score: ___ /35

1 **Read. Then complete. (6 points)**

> ahead   front   office   road   second   stop

How do you get to the post ^{1}_____? Start at your house and go straight ^{2}_____.

Turn right in ^{3}_____ of the café. Take the ^{4}_____ next to the bus ^{5}_____ and

walk to the end of the road. Take the ^{6}_____ road on the left.

2 **Look at the map. Then read and write. (14 points)**

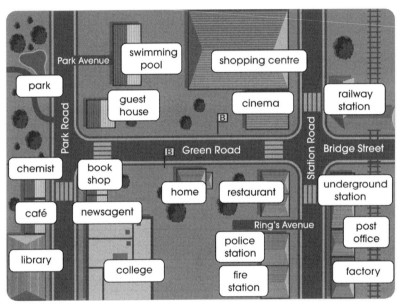

1 Start at the police station. Turn right into Ring's Avenue and go straight ahead. Turn left into Station Road, and go straight ahead. It's the first building on the left.

It's the _____.

2 Start at the shopping centre. Turn right into Station Road and then turn right into Green Road. Go straight ahead to the end of the road and turn right into Park Road. Take the first road on the right.

It's the _____.

3 Start at the library. _____

_____.

It's the post office.

4 Start at the underground station. _____

_____.

It's the college.

Score: ____ /20

1 **Listen. Then match. (5 points)**

1	The supermarket is ...	**a**	between the bookshop and the chemist.
2	The newsagent's is ...	**b**	near here.
3	The station is ...	**c**	in front of the bus stop.
4	The college is ...	**d**	over the bridge.
5	The post office isn't ...	**e**	next to the swimming pool.

2 **Listen and circle. (5 points)**

1 If the weather is good, we can go to the (park / stadium).

2 I can go to the (cinema / theatre) if I'm not too tired.

3 If you're ill, you should go to the (chemist's / doctor's).

4 If you want to have fun, (you / we) can go to the circus.

5 If you finish your homework, you (can / should) come to the shopping centre.

3 **Look at the map. Then talk. (5 points)**

- Is/Are there ...?
- How do you get to the ...?
- If you ...
- It's on the corner/at the end/in front of ...

Score: ____ /15

Whole test score: ____ /35

1 **Read. Then complete. (6 points)** | dishes food had made read turned |

Yesterday I made curry with my friend Alina. First, we ¹_____ a list of ingredients, then we bought the ²_____ in the supermarket. Next, we ³_____ the recipe. I ⁴_____ on the oven and cooked the stew. After an hour, it was finished. Then Alina's mum and dad came home and we all ⁵_____ a meal. It was delicious! Last, we washed the ⁶_____.

2 **Read. Then write T = True or F = False. (6 points)**

I'm Caroline. Last night, I went to my friend Tina's house. We watched two films and played computer games. It was great. Tina's dad cooked chicken. I had a very big plate because I love it, but I was taking my dinner to the living room when … oh no! I dropped the plate. There was food everywhere! It made me very sad because Tina's dad was cooking for hours. I helped clean the food up. Tina's dad was great. He gave me some more chicken. Later in the evening, Tina's mum came home from work. She wanted to have dinner. Her dad looked in the pan. There was no more chicken because I ate it. I ate it because I dropped mine. Now I feel really, really sad.

1 Caroline went to the cinema. ☐

2 Caroline likes chicken very much. ☐

3 They ate the chicken in the kitchen. ☐

4 Caroline helped clean up. ☐

5 Tina's dad was angry. ☐

6 Tina's mum didn't have any chicken. ☐

3 **Read the text again. Then answer. (4 points)**

1 What did Caroline and Tina do? _____

2 Why did Caroline have a big plate of chicken? _____

3 Who did Caroline help? _____

4 Why did Tina's mum not have chicken? _____

4 **What happened? Write. (4 points)** | make buy wash serve |

1 _____

2 _____

3 _____

4 _____

Score: ___ /20

 PHOTOCOPIABLE

 Listen. Then tick (✓). (8 points)

Tom's list			
banana		jam	
beans		omlette	
biscuits		rice	
cake		salad	
cheese		spaghetti	
chicken		sugar	
chips		sweets	
fish			

Sarah's list			
banana		jam	
beans		omlette	
biscuits		rice	
cake		salad	
cheese		soup	
chicken		spaghetti	
chips		sugar	
fish			

Listen. Then write _T = True_ or _F = False_. (6 points)

1 Debbie didn't have a good day yesterday. ☐

2 It was her dad's birthday. ☐

3 She made a list. ☐

4 She didn't buy the ingredients. ☐

5 Her friend prepared the ingredients. ☐

6 Debbie's dad washed the dishes. ☐

A happy day. Make notes. Then talk. (6 points)

- What happened?
- I went/saw/played/bought/had …

- I didn't …
- It made me …

_____

_____

_____

_____

Score: ____ /20

Whole test score: ____ /40

1 Read. Then complete. (6 points)

had   list   oven   prepared   recipe   washed

Yesterday I made rice and beans with my friend Harry. First, we made a ¹_____ of ingredients, then we bought the food in the supermarket. Next, we read the ²_____, then we ³_____ the ingredients. I turned on the ⁴_____ and cooked the rice and beans. After an hour, it was finished. Then Harry's family came home and we all ⁵_____ a meal. It was delicious! Last, we ⁶_____ the dishes.

2 Read. Then write the order. (6 points)

I'm George. Yesterday was a good day. I got up at seven o'clock in the morning. The sky was blue and the sun was shining. I packed my bag and went to the bus stop. The bus came and I went to the sports centre. My friend, Tom was there. He was playing volleyball in the gym when I arrived. I went to the swimming pool and swam for two hours. I was very tired. At lunch time, I met Tom in the café at the sports centre and we had lunch. We ate chicken curry and rice. We had some fruit juice to drink and then we had an ice cream. We walked back to my house and played on my new computer all afternoon. It was great.

a George met Tom for lunch. ☐

b The bus came. ☐

c They played on the computer. ☐

d George packed his bag. ☐

e George was tired. ☐

f They had chicken curry and rice. ☐

3 Read the text again. Then answer. (4 points)

1 Was Tom in the sports centre?   _____

2 Why was George tired?   _____

3 What did they have for lunch?   _____

4 Whose computer did they play with?   _____

4 What happened? Write. (4 points)

make   read   prepare   have

1 _____

2 _____

3 _____

4 _____

Score: ___ /20

4 **Good food, good mood**

1 🎧 **10** **Listen. Then complete. (8 points)**

Tom had ¹_____ and ²_____ to start with. Then Tom had ³_____
and ⁴_____. Sarah's mum made Thai ⁵_____ and ⁶_____. Sarah didn't
have any biscuits or ⁷_____. She had salad and a ⁸_____.

2 🎧 **11** **Listen. Then write T = True or F = False. (6 points)**

1 Debbie had a good day yesterday. ☐

2 She forgot her shopping list. ☐

3 Her friend didn't want to help. ☐

4 Debbie prepared the ingredients. ☐

5 They both washed the dishes. ☐

6 Debbie's dad wasn't happy. ☐

3 **A day where everything went wrong. Make notes. Then talk. (6 points)**

- What happened?
- I played/went/forgot …
- I didn't … because …
- It made me …

_____

_____

_____

_____

_____

_____

Score: ___ /20

Whole test score: ___ /40

1 Read. Then complete. (4 points)   comedy   fantasy   thriller   sci-fi

1 Watch this _____ about a scary house in the mountains.

2 In this _____ film, monkeys go into space.

3 Laugh at Bill and Joe as they chase the diamond thieves in this _____.

4 Follow Emma Hill in this _____ film where she meets unusual creatures.

2 Look and complete. Then answer for you. (8 points)

1 Have you ever (play)   _____? _____.

2 Have you ever (go to)   _____? _____.

3 Have you ever (play)   _____? _____.

4 Have you ever (listen to)   _____? _____.

3 Read. Then write *T = True* or *F = False*. (4 points)

Jane: Have you ever played a saxophone, Linda?

Linda: No, I haven't but my brother has. Have you?

Jane: Yes, I have. I have lessons every week.

Linda: How long have you played the saxophone?

Jane: I've played it for two years. I love it.

Linda: Have you ever played in front of your school?

Jane: No, I'm too embarrassed, but I've played in front of my family and friends!

Linda: Really? I love playing the clarinet in front of my school.

1 Jane's brother has played the saxophone. ☐

2 Jane has played the saxophone for two years. ☐

3 Jane hasn't played the saxophone in front of her family. ☐

4 Linda dislikes the clarinet. ☐

4 Read. Then complete. (4 points)

1 Dan _____ (not do) his homework yet.

2 My sister _____ (never make) a cake.

3 We _____ (live) in our house for five years.

4 I _____ (already seen) this film.

Score: ____ /20

1 **Listen and write. (6 points)**

1 Have you ever _____ the harp, Christine?

2 Steve, have your mum and dad _____ to your brother playing the trumpet in a concert?

3 Karen, has your sister _____ the triangle?

4 Have you _____ my harmonica, Tom?

5 Has Bob _____ a saxophone?

6 Have you ever _____ the drums, Ron?

2 **Listen. Then write T = True or F = False. (8 points)**

1 Zoe went to two concerts last week. ☐

2 She heard a girl play the harp in the first concert. ☐

3 The girl played very quickly. ☐

4 There was a boy who played the cello. ☐

5 The second concert was a band of six people. ☐

6 The band played jazz and folk music. ☐

7 There were two men playing saxophones. ☐

8 Zoe couldn't see the man who was singing. ☐

3 **Describe this picture. Write notes. Then talk. (6 points)**

- What music …?
- Which instruments …?
- How many …?
- Have you ever …?

_____

_____

_____

_____

_____

_____

Score: ____ /20

Whole test score: ____ /40

1 Read. Then complete. (4 points) biography cartoon musical romance

1 Sing and dance with the children from High School Musical in this _____.

2 Follow the adventures of these cute animals in this _____ with beautiful drawings.

3 Pablo falls in love with the beautiful Princess Lee in this _____.

4 Learn about the life of Queen Elizabeth I in this _____.

2 Put the words in order to make questions. Then answer for you. (8 points)

1 ever / thriller / have / a / you / seen

_____ ? _____ .

2 tambourine / have / ever / the / you / played

_____ ? _____ .

3 you / long / in / have / your / lived / house / how

_____ ? _____ .

4 drawn / have / ever / a / you / cartoon

_____ ? _____ .

3 Read Fiona's story. Then write T = True or F = False. (4 points)

Have you ever seen a really scary film? I have. It was a Friday evening. I went to the cinema with some friends. We went to see a thriller. I didn't want to go because I don't like scary films, but my friends wanted to go. The first 30 minutes were OK. Then it started to get really scary. I hid my face behind my hands. I could hear the music. It was really loud. Then it went really quiet. I looked through my fingers at my friends. They were sitting on their chairs. Then there was a loud noise and everyone screamed. I got up and ran out of the cinema. I phoned my dad. I've never been so happy to go home!

1 The film was a comedy. ☐

2 Fiona disliked the film. ☐

3 Fiona wasn't watching the film for the first 30 minutes. ☐

4 Fiona left the cinema and called her dad. ☐

4 Read. Then complete. (4 points)

1 Dan _____ (live) in his house since 2012.

2 Ana _____ (never eat) paella.

3 I _____ (not do) my homework yet.

4 I _____ (already make) my bed.

Score: ____ /20

Listen. Then write T = True or F = False. (6 points)

1 Christine wants to learn to play the harp. ☐

2 Steve's parents have listened to him play the trumpet. ☐

3 Karen's sister hasn't found the triangle. ☐

4 Tom hasn't seen Jim's harmonica. ☐

5 Bob has bought a saxophone. ☐

6 Ron hasn't played the drums. ☐

  Listen. Then write. (8 points)

| cello   classical   drums   harmonica   piano   saxophones   tambourine   triangle |

Hi. I'm Zoe. I love music. Last week, I went to two concerts. They were great. In the first concert, I heard a girl play the ^{1}_____. She was ten. I've never heard anyone play the piano that young. Her fingers played so quickly. She played ^{2}_____ music. Then there was a boy who was twelve. He played the ^{3}_____. Have you ever played the cello? It doesn't look easy.

The second concert was very different. It was a band. There were six men in the band. They played some reggae music and disco. I've never been to such a noisy concert! One man played the ^{4}_____. Two men were playing ^{5}_____. I love the saxophone. I want to play the saxophone one day. Then there was a man on the ^{6}_____. One man in the band was playing a ^{7}_____ and a ^{8}_____, but I couldn't see him. And … the sixth man in the band was singing.

 Have you ever been to a concert? Write notes in your notebook. Then talk. (6 points)

- Where was it?
- Which instruments did you hear?
- Have you ever …?

Score: ____ /20

Whole test score: ____ /40

1 **Read. Then match. (4 points)**

1 What will you do tomorrow, Anna?   **a** I'll look at the plants and flowers.

2 What will you do at the botanical gardens?   **b** I'll look for the biggest fish.

3 What will you do at the museum?   **c** I'll see the dinosaurs.

4 What will you do at the aquarium?   **d** First, I'll go to the castle.

2 **Put the words in order to make sentences. Then number the sentences in order. (8 points)**

1 It's / sure / not / . / very / I'm / expensive _____. ☐

2 good / a / that's / idea _____! ☐

3 go / the / to / palace / could / we _____. ☐

4 else / what / we / could / do _____? ☐

3 **Read Sally's day out. Then answer. (4 points)**

I'm going to a theme park tomorrow with my friends. I'm really excited! I want to go on all the rides. In the morning, I'll go on the pirate ship first. Then, I'll play mini-golf. Next, I'll go on the dodgems. I love the dodgems. Then, I'll go on the carousel. After that, I'll have lunch. After lunch, I'll go on the boating lake and then the water slide. And last, I'll go on the rollercoaster. What else could I do? Oh, yes. I could go on the big wheel!

1 Where's Sally going to go? _____.

2 What will she do first? _____.

3 What will she do after lunch? _____.

4 If Sally has time, what else could she do? _____.

4 **Make plans. Complete the conversation. (4 points)**

Steve: Hi, Tina! ¹_____ Natural History museum?

Tina: I think it's closed today.

Steve: OK, shall we go hiking in the National Park?

Tina: ²_____.

Steve: That's a pity. I love hiking.

Tina: ³_____?

Steve: We could go to the palace.

Tina: ⁴_____. Let's do that.

Score: ____ /20

1 **Listen. Then write T = True or F = False. (5 points)**

1 Rachel doesn't want to go to the theme park. ☐

2 Tim wants to go to the water park. ☐

3 Rachel can't swim. ☐

4 Rachel loves visiting castles. ☐

5 They will go to the museum. ☐

2 **Listen. Then write. (6 points)**

At the theme park, Jan will …

1 go on the _____.

2 go on the _____.

3 go on the _____.

4 go on the _____.

5 go on the _____.

6 play _____.

3 **Think of a summer holiday. Make notes. Then talk. (9 points)**

Score: ____ /20

Whole test score: ____ /40

1 **Read. Then match. (4 points)**

1 What will you do tomorrow, Pete?
2 What will you do at the National Park
3 What will you do at the palace?
4 What will you do at the theme park?

a I think I'll go to the theme park.
b I'll visit the Queen!
c I'll go on the big wheel.
d I'll go hiking and look for animals.

2 **Put the words in order to make sentences. Then complete the conversation. (8 points)**

Jules: ¹_____?

Drew: ²_____.
What will we do if it rains?

Jules: We could go to the museum.

Drew: ³_____.

Jules: ⁴_____.
Have you been there?

Drew: No, I haven't.

a last / went / weekend / no / I
b sure / not / I'm
c in / National / the / go / shall / Park / hiking / we / tomorrow
d castle / to / could / the / go / we

3 **Read Gemma's plan. Then write. (4 points)**

Tomorrow, I want to go to the museum. Mum wants to go with me. Dad can't go. He's got a lot of work to do. First: dinosaurs. I love studying them. Then I'll look at the fossils. There are lots of fossils of sea animals and plants in the museum. I've never seen a fossil! After the fossils, I could go to see the pirate treasure. The treasure was found near our town last year. It was under the sea for three hundred years. Last month, they put it in the museum. Then, if I've got time, I'll go to the theatre. There's a model of an old, Italian theatre in the museum. The original is over two thousand years old! It'll be an amazing day!

1 Why isn't Dad going to the museum? _____.

2 What does Gemma love studying? _____.

3 What will Gemma see after the dinosaurs? _____.

4 If Gemma has time, what will she do? _____.

4 **Make plans. Complete the conversation. (4 points)**

Adam: Hi, Maya! ¹_____?

Maya: Oh, I'm not sure. I think it's closed today.

Adam: OK, ²_____?

Maya: I don't like hiking. What else could we do?

Adam: ³_____.

Maya: That's a great idea! ⁴_____.

Score: ___ /20

1 Listen. Then tick or cross. (5 points)

1 shopping centre ☐
2 water park ☐
3 castle ☐
4 theme park ☐
5 museum ☐

2 Listen. Then number in the correct order. (6 points)

Today, Jan will ...

a go on the dodgems. ☐
b go on the pirate ship. ☐
c go on the big wheel. ☐
d go on the boating lake. ☐
e go on the rollercoaster. ☐
f play mini golf. ☐

3 Think of a winter holiday. Make notes. Then talk. (9 points)

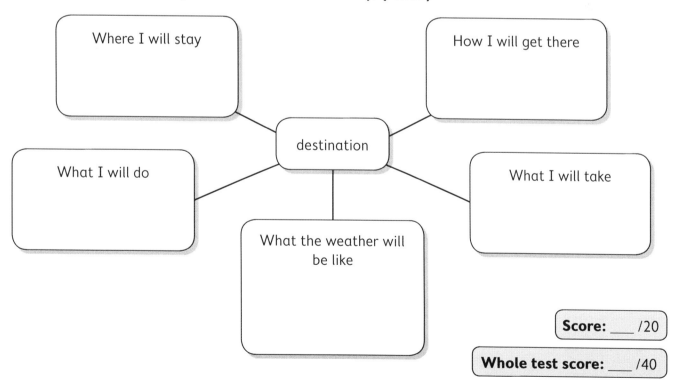

Where I will stay

How I will get there

What I will do

destination

What I will take

What the weather will be like

Score: ___ /20

Whole test score: ___ /40

1 Put the words in order to make sentences. (6 points)

1 do / space / to / in / need / astronauts / exercise

_____.

2 the / look / directly / shouldn't / sun / you / at

_____.

3 your / had / tonight / better / homework / do / you

_____.

4 for / Joe / to / out / his / about / Mars / find / project / needs

_____.

5 bedroom / tidy / ought / you / to / your

_____.

6 watch / aliens / that / should / about / we / film

_____.

2 Read. Then write T = True or F = False. (6 points)

I'm Jackie. My dad says that he's got one of the most complicated telescopes. It's really big. He keeps it in our attic. There's a window in the attic and you can see the stars through it. Some nights, when there aren't any clouds, you can see stars and planets and comets. It's amazing! I'm always asking my dad 'Which star is the closest?' or 'Which planet is the most interesting?'. I love asking questions. My dad is brilliant! He knows the answer to every question!

Tonight, Dad wants to take the telescope outside because we can see more. He says it isn't very cold, but I should put a coat on. He says we will see more planets and stars if we go outside. Right! I'd better get my jacket and boots on. Looking at the stars is the best way to learn about space.

1 Jackie's dad's telescope isn't very complicated. ☐

2 Jackie isn't interested in space. ☐

3 Every night is cloudy. ☐

4 Dad answers all the questions. ☐

5 They go outside because they will see more stars outside. ☐

6 Jackie wants to put her jacket and boots on because it's very cold outside. ☐

3 Imagine a planet. Then write what it would be like. (8 points)

_____

_____

_____

_____

Score: ___ /20

© Pearson Education Limited 2018   PHOTOCOPIABLE

1 **Listen. Then write T = True or F = False. (7 points)**

1 Charlie's dad shows him the different planets. ☐

2 His dad has got a new rocket. ☐

3 Charlie is reading a story about a new planet. ☐

4 The alien meets an astronaut. ☐

5 The alien has got a big rocket. ☐

6 They travel together. ☐

7 The alien and astronaut don't see any comets. ☐

2 **Listen. Then write. (6 points)**

> astronaut   film   journey   photograph   story   telescope

1 interesting   _____

2 amazing   _____

3 expensive   _____

4 horrible   _____

5 frightening   _____

6 important   _____

3 **Choose one picture and describe it. Can your teacher guess which picture you are describing? (7 points)**

- What's it like?
- What / Who lives there?
- Is it amazing/interesting/complicated ...?

Score: ____ /20

Whole test score: ____ /40

1 **Put the words in order to make sentences. (6 points)**

1 bedroom / tidy / your / dinner / had / you / after / better

_____.

2 the / to / call / ought / police / we

_____.

3 should / teacher / to / Harry / the / listen

_____.

4 our / astronauts / for / need / we / about / homework / write / to

_____.

5 grandparents / visit / my / ought / to / I

_____.

6 take / telescope / need / to / Dad / his / doesn't

_____.

2 **Read. Then write. (6 points)**

I'm Jackie. My dad says that he's got one of the most complicated telescopes. It's really big. He keeps it in our attic. There's a window in the attic and you can see the stars through it. Some nights, when there aren't any clouds, you can see stars and planets and comets. It's amazing! I'm always asking my dad 'Which star is the closest?' or 'Which planet is the most interesting?'. I love asking questions. My dad is brilliant! He knows the answer to every question!

Tonight, Dad wants to take the telescope outside because we can see more. He says it isn't very cold, but I should put a coat on. He says we will see more planets and stars if we go outside. Right! I'd better get my jacket and boots on. Looking at the stars is the best way to learn about space.

1 Whose is the telescope? _____.

2 Why is the telescope good? _____.

3 What can Jackie see when it isn't cloudy? _____.

4 What is Jackie's dad like? _____.

5 What should Jackie do before going outside? _____.

6 What's the best way to learn about space? _____.

3 **Imagine a planet. Then write what it would be like. (8 points)**

_____

_____

_____

Score: ____ /20

7 Space

1 **Listen. Then complete. (7 points)**

> alien   astronaut   comets   planets   rocket   spaceship   telescope

I love looking at the stars. My dad shows me the different [1]_____ I can't remember all of them. I should draw them in a notebook and write the names next to them. Tonight, we're going to look at Mars. My Dad's got a new [2]_____ and he wants to use it. We should see some of the planets that are closer to Earth.
I love reading sci-fi stories, too. I'm reading a story about an [3]_____ from Mars. He meets an [4]_____ in space. The alien goes into the astronaut's [5]_____, but the rocket isn't very big. The alien has got a [6]_____. It's bigger than the rocket. He invites the astronaut to his spaceship. And ... They travel through space together and see different stars, planets and [7]_____. They have lots of adventures. Oh ... I'd better get ready. I need to put on some warm clothes because it might be cold outside tonight. My dad's got the telescope ready. Coming, Dad!

2 **Listen. Then match. (6 points)**

1	interesting	**a**	telescope
2	amazing	**b**	astronaut
3	expensive	**c**	photograph
4	horrible	**d**	story
5	frightening	**e**	film
6	important	**f**	journey

3 **Choose one picture and describe it. Can your teacher guess which picture you are describing? (7 points)**

- What's it like?
- Is it amazing/interesting/complicated ...?

- What/Who lives there?

Score: ___ /20

Whole test score: ___ /40

1 Read. Then match. (4 points)

1	plenty	**a**	a bottle of cola
2	a few	**b**	sugar
3	half	**c**	tomatoes
4	a little	**d**	of cake

2 Complete. Then match. (10 points)

1 If you _____ ,

2 If you _____ ,

3 If you _____ ,

4 If you _____ ,

5 If you _____ ,

a you'll keep the planet clean.

b you'll reduce pollution.

c you'll conserve energy.

d you'll save trees.

e you'll reduce waste.

3 Read. Then write T = True or F = False. (6 points)

Hi. I'm Jake. There are a few things my family can do to protect the environment. I've got a timetable with jobs for everyone in my family. Every week, we're going to do different jobs and help each other. The first job I'm going to do is to collect rubbish. I'm going to collect rubbish in my bedroom and in the house and I'm going to help collect rubbish in the park. Mum's first job is to help save trees. She's going to recycle paper. Every day she uses a lot of paper and now she's going to stop. Dad's going to reduce pollution. He always goes to work by car because it's quicker and easier, but now he's going to get the train. My brother, Freddie is going to go round the house and turn off all the lights. He's going to conserve energy, and my little sister, Patsy is going to reuse plastic bags. She's going to put the plastic bags in the car when Mum goes shopping. What are you going to do to help?

1 Jake is going to do different jobs to help the environment. ☐

2 Jake's going to tidy the bedrooms. ☐

3 Mum always recycles paper. ☐

4 Dad is going to use public transport to go to work. ☐

5 Freddie is going to turn off the lights. ☐

6 Patsy is going to buy plastic bags. ☐

Score: ____ /20

1 **Listen. Then number in the correct order. (6 points)**

a recycle paper ☐

b turn off the lights ☐

c collect rubbish ☐

d reuse plastic bags ☐

e use public transport ☐

f recycle bottles ☐

2 **Listen. Then write _T = True_ or _F = False_. (6 points)**

1 Jenny is going to turn on the lights. ☐

2 Steve is going to put rubbish in his bedroom in the bin. ☐

3 Hilary is going to reduce waste by reusing plastic bottles. ☐

4 Tony is going to recycle empty bottles. ☐

5 Ed is going to recycle paper to help save rainforests. ☐

6 Vicky is going to go to school by bus. ☐

3 **How do you help to protect the environment? Make notes. Then talk. (8 points)**

- I always/sometimes/often … because …
- If I …
- If I don't …
- I can/can't …

_____

_____

_____

_____

_____

_____

_____

_____

Score: ___ /20

Whole test score: ___ /40

1 **Read. Then match. (4 points)**

1 plenty	**2** a little	**3** half	**4** a few
a a glass of water	**b** bananas	**c** of vinegar	**d** salt

2 **Read. Then match. (10 points)**

1	If you recycle	a	the lights,	A	you'll keep the planet clean.
2	If you collect	b	paper,	B	you'll reduce pollution.
3	If you reuse	c	public transport,	C	you'll reduce waste.
4	If you turn off	d	rubbish,	D	you'll conserve energy.
5	If you use	e	bottles,	E	you'll save trees.

3 **Read. Then answer. (6 points)**

Hi. I'm Mary and I'm doing a project to find out what we can do to help protect the environment. What can we do? First, we can help by collecting rubbish. Do you collect all your rubbish and put it in the bin? If we collect rubbish, we'll keep the planet clean and you can help. If you see rubbish in the playground or in the park, put it in the bin. Second, we can help by using public transport. How do you get to school? Do you go by car? If we use public transport, we'll reduce pollution and the world will be cleaner. Third, we can help by reusing plastic bags. How many plastic bags do you take to the supermarket? If we reuse plastic bags, we'll reduce waste. Keep plastic bags in your bag or in the car to use next time you go shopping with your mum and dad. Fourth, we can help by turning off the lights. Do you turn off the light when you leave your bedroom? If we turn off the lights, we'll conserve energy. Fifth, we can help by recycling bottles. Does your family recycle bottles? If we recycle bottles, we can save resources. And sixth, we can recycle paper. Do you write on all the paper you use? If we recycle paper, we can save trees. Make a recycling box in your house and at school and get recycling!

1 What should you do if you see rubbish in the playground?

_____

2 What can we do to reduce pollution?

_____

3 Where can we keep plastic bags?

_____

4 What happens when you turn off lights?

_____

5 How can we save resources?

_____

6 How can we save trees?

_____

Score: ____ /20

1 Listen. Then write *T* = *True* or *F* = *False*. **(6 points)**

1 Kelly is going to ride her bike to school or catch the bus. ☐

2 Her dad is going to recycle glass bottles. ☐

3 On Wednesday, Kelly is going to collect rubbish in the park. ☐

4 Kelly is going to recycle paper. ☐

5 She is going to turn on all the lights. ☐

6 Kelly and her parents are going to reuse plastic bags when they go shopping. ☐

2 Listen. Then match. **(6 points)**

1	Jenny	**a**	recycle paper
2	Steve	**b**	turn off the lights
3	Hilary	**c**	use public transport
4	Tony	**d**	reuse plastic bags
5	Ed	**e**	recycle bottles
6	Vicky	**f**	collect the rubbish

3 What happens if you protect the environment? Make notes. Then talk. **(8 points)**

- I ... because ...
- If we ...
- If we don't ...
- I can/can't ...

_____

_____

_____

_____

_____

_____

_____

Score: ____ /20

Whole test score: ____ /40

End of term 1

1 **Read. Then match. (7 points)**

1	What can you do at the campsite?	**a**	It's four hundred kilogrammes.
2	Can you light a fire?	**b**	It's the blue whale.
3	How heavy is it?	**c**	Turn left and go straight ahead. It's on the left.
4	How tall is it?	**d**	You can swim in the river, or light a fire.
5	Was the elephant taller than the giraffe?	**e**	It's three metres fifty.
6	Which is the heaviest animal?	**f**	No, I can't.
7	How do you get to the post office?	**g**	No, it wasn't.

2 **Look and read. Then match. (6 points)**

1 What are you doing, Alex and Irene? We're pitching the tent.

2 What is Clara doing? She's lighting a campfire.

3 Are giraffes taller than camels? Yes, they are.

4 Where is the newsagent's? It's between the bookshop and the guest house.

5 Where is the bus stop? It's on the corner of the road.

6 Which is the smallest – the otter or the whale? The otter is.

 a
 b
 c
 d
 e
 f

3 **Read. Then circle. (7 points)**

1 I like (go / going) hiking, but I (don't / doesn't) like sailing.

2 He is (put / putting) in the pegs.

3 What is she (do / doing)? She is (pitch / pitching) the tent.

4 We're good at (dancing / dance). We practise every day.

5 The hippo is the (heavy / heaviest) animal.

6 The giraffe is the (taller / tallest).

7 If you (want / wanting) to take a bus, you must (go / going) to the bus stop.

 PHOTOCOPIABLE

End of term 1

4 Read. Then complete. (11 points)

between   camping   cinema   fire   fossils   heaviest   pitched   put in   saw   sang   taller

I'm on a school trip with my class. It's great! We're ¹_____ on a campsite near the beach.

When we got here, we ²_____ the tents. I helped to ³_____ the pegs. After dinner,

we lit a ⁴_____ and we sat round it and ⁵_____ songs. We had lots of fun. Today we

went to the zoo. We ⁶_____ some elephants and giraffes. The giraffes were ⁷_____

than the elephants, but the elephants were the ⁸_____ animals in the zoo. Tomorrow we're

going to look for ⁹_____ on the beach. Then we're going to the Natural History museum.

It's ¹⁰_____ the ¹¹_____ and the shopping centre.

5 How do you get to the … from the post office? Write directions. (9 points)

at the end of   behind   between   in front of   near   next to   straight ahead

1 factory: _____

_____

2 guest house: _____

_____

3 college: _____

_____

guest house

sports centre

Park Street

London Road

Station Road

factory

college

chemist

bookshop

cinema

post office

circus

shopping centre

Score: ____ /40

1 Listen. Then complete. (20 points)

Wendy

I'm ¹_____. I love ²_____. At the moment, I'm putting in the tent ³_____. After that, I'm ⁴_____ a campfire. I love campfires. Tomorrow morning, we're taking ⁵_____ the tents. Then we're hiking fifteen kilometres. We're hiking to a big ⁶_____ next to the ⁷_____. It's very quiet.

Sebastian

I'm ⁸_____. I love ⁹_____, but I don't like ¹⁰_____. At the moment, I'm on a fishing trip on a ¹¹_____! It's ¹²_____ and I'm wet and cold. I want to keep out of the ¹³_____. We've got a small, green ¹⁴_____. I can ¹⁵_____ the tent. Then I'll be warm and dry!

Martin

I'm eleven. I love ¹⁶_____. I've got a small grey and green ¹⁷_____. In my rucksack, I've got a blue ¹⁸_____, a ¹⁹_____ and my climbing shoes. Tomorrow morning, we're climbing a mountain next to the ²⁰_____. I'm very excited but a little scared!

2 Listen. Then write. (5 points)

How heavy/long is it?

1 _____ kilogrammes

2 _____ kilogrammes

3 _____ kilogrammes

4 _____ metres

5 _____ metres

3 **Listen. Then number in the correct order. (12 points)**

1 The stadium

a Go past the fire station and turn right at the bus stop. ☐

b The stadium is directly in front of you. ☐

c Then turn left. ☐

d Continue straight ahead to a big guest house. ☐

e Turn right here. ☐

f Go straight ahead to the end of the road. ☐

2 The bookshop

a Go across the road and continue straight ahead. ☐

b The bookshop is opposite the station. ☐

c At the traffic lights turn left. ☐

d When you can see the university, turn right. ☐

e Continue along this road to the railway station. ☐

f Go to the end of the road. ☐

4 **Look at the animals. Then talk. (8 points)**

- It's a ...
- It's ... metres tall/long.
- It's ... kilogrammes.
- The ... is taller/shorter than the ....

- The ... is heavier/lighter than the ....
- The ... is the tallest animal.
- The ... is the heaviest animal.

Score: ___ /45

Whole test score: ___ /85

1 **Read. Then match. (8 points)**

1	What happened?	a	No, she hasn't.
2	Did you watch the film by yourself?	b	We missed the bus.
3	How long has Tim been playing the drums?	c	I'll visit the museum.
4	Have you ever played the saxophone?	d	Yes, I did.
5	Has Margaret heard the song yet?	e	I'm not sure.
6	What will you do tomorrow?	f	Yes, I have.
7	Shall we go to the castle?	g	We could go to the water park.
8	What else could we do?	h	For two years.

2 **Read. Then match. (6 points)**

1 I watched a thriller on TV yesterday.
2 I was in the tent while it was raining.
3 Have you heard a harp?
4 He has just passed his test.
5 Shall we go on the big wheel?
6 I'll go to the castle next weekend.

3 **Read. Then answer for you. (6 points)**

1 What will you do at the weekend? _____.

2 What else could you do? _____.

3 Have you ever listened to jazz music? _____.

4 Have you ever played in a concert? _____.

5 How long have you been in your class? _____.

6 What happened at school yesterday? _____.

 PHOTOCOPIABLE

End of term 2

4 **Read and complete the table. Then match. (22 points)**

thriller   jazz   country   musical   blues

cartoon   rock   romance   sci-fi   pop   comedy

a   b

music	films

c    d

e

k

f   g    h    i    j

5 **Write about last night. What did you do? (8 points)**

- What happened last night?
- Where were you?
- I was ... when ...

- I/We played/watched/listened to ...
- I ... by myself.

_____

_____

_____

_____

_____

_____

Score: ____ /50

1 Listen. Then number in the correct order. (6 points)

a I cooked the tomatoes. ☐

b The plate fell onto the floor. ☐

c I boiled water and cooked pasta. ☐

d I put pasta on a plate. ☐

e I cooked chicken and rice. ☐

f I cut some tomatoes in half. ☐

2 Listen and circle. (7 points)

1 Richard was (ill / tired).

2 His team (played / were playing) football.

3 It (was / wasn't) an important game.

4 Richard (hasn't been / has been) to the doctor's.

5 Richard's sister is called (Ellie / Emma).

6 A friend brought some (books / films) for Richard.

7 He didn't have dinner because (Mum dropped the spaghetti / he wasn't hungry).

3 Listen. Then match. (6 points)

1 palace   **a** boating lake

2 museum   **b** rollercoaster

3 water park   **c** pirate ship

4 castle   **d** dodgems

5 aquarium   **e** carousel

6 theme park   **f** mini-golf

4 Look and read. Answer and ask questions with your teacher. (10 points)

1

Question	Answer
Name / restaurant?	
What type / food / have?	
Who / eat there?	
Where / restaurant?	
How many stars / got?	

2

Question	Answer
Name / restaurant?	Curry World.
What type / food / have?	Hot curries!
Who / eat there?	The Ball family.
Where / restaurant?	In the square.
How many stars / got?	★★★★★

5 Think about a good day and a bad day. Then talk. (6 points)

- What happened?
- I went to …
- I saw/played …
- I ate …
- It was a good day because …

A bad day:
- What happened?
- I went to …
- I fell/dropped …
- I didn't eat …
- It was a bad day because …

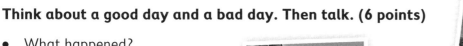

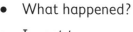

Score: ____ /35

Whole test score: ____ /85

1 **Read. Then complete. (8 points)**

going   most   ought   rubbish   recycle   what   which   you

1 _____ planet is that? It's the red planet.

2 It's cold. You _____ to put on your jacket.

3 Which telescope is the _____ complicated? The newest one is.

4 Are _____ going to help? Yes, I am.

5 _____ can you do to help? I can collect _____.

6 I'm _____ to _____ paper.

2 **Read and write complete sentences. Then match. (12 points)**

1 comet / more / interesting / planet

_____.

2 big telescope / complicated / small telescope

_____.

3 I / going / recycle bottles

_____.

4 she / going / recycle / paper

_____.

5 they / going / use / public transport

_____.

6 green alien / frightening / yellow alien

_____.

(a)

(b)

(c)

(f)

(e)

(d)

3 Put the words in order to make sentences. (6 points)

1 hat / cold / because / should / a / it's / you / wear

_____.

2 go / inside / better / had / we

_____.

3 look / stars / ought / to / they / at / the

_____.

4 spaceship / amazing / white / the / the / most / is

_____.

5 very / astronomer / interesting / the / is

_____.

6 day / decided / go / hot / one / swimming / to / we

_____.

4 Read. Then match. (6 points)

1 If you recycle paper …

2 If you use public transport …

3 If you turn off the lights …

4 You'll reduce waste …

5 You'll save resources …

6 You'll keep the planet clean …

a you'll conserve energy.

b if you reuse plastic bags.

c if you collect rubbish.

d you'll save trees.

e you'll reduce pollution.

f if you recycle bottles.

5 Write about our planet. (8 points)

- What are you going to do to protect the planet?
- We/You/I should/ought to/had better …

- I'm going to …

_____

_____

_____

_____

Score: ____ /40

1 **Listen. Then circle. (8 points)**

1 Tim is reading a book about an (alien / astronaut).

2 The alien's really (intelligent / interesting).

3 The alien in the book visits lots of different (comets / planets).

4 The book is like a (funny / frightening) sci-fi film.

5 The boy uses his Dad's (complicated / expensive) telescope to look at the night sky.

6 They (have / haven't) seen the star before.

7 The boy and dad should get ready for (aliens / monsters).

8 Tim (tells / doesn't tell) us the end of the story.

2   **Listen. Then tick (✓). (6 points)**

1 collect rubbish ☐   **2** recycle bottles ☐

3 recycle paper ☐   **4** reuse plastic bags ☐

5 use public transport ☐   **6** turn off the lights ☐

3   **Listen. Then complete. (5 points)**

1 Name: Valentina _____

2 Name of rocket: _____

3 Date the rocket launched: _____ 1963

4 How many days in space: _____ days

5 Number of times round Earth: _____

End of term 3

4 Look and read. Answer and ask questions with your teacher. (10 points)

1

Question	Answer
Name / astronaut?	
Where / he/she / go?	
Name / rocket?	
What / he/she / see?	
When / he/she / go?	

2

Question	Answer
Name / astronaut?	Astrid Mars
Where / he/she / go?	The Moon
Name / rocket?	Challenger 99
What / he/she / see?	volcanoes
When / he/she / go?	on 10th December

5 Think about how you can help the environment. Then talk. (6 points)

- I recycle …
- I use …

- I collect …
- I reuse …

- I take …

6 Look at the story. Then say what is happening. (10 points)

Jake and the lost spaceship.

One day in April last year, a spaceship landed in a field. It was only four o'clock in the morning, but the noise and the lights woke Jake up. He looked out of his bedroom window. **Now, YOU tell the story.**

① ② ③ ④ ⑤

Score: ____ /45

Whole test score: ____ /85

 Read. Then circle. (5 points)

Beth – the tour guide

This month, I am going to talk to some people about their jobs. I want to find out where they live, what they like about their job and a little more information about their lives. This is Beth. Beth is a tour guide. She lives in a rural area in the south of England but she works all over the world.

Bob: What do you like about your job, Beth?

Beth: I love visiting different countries and I love talking to people.

Bob: What tours do you do?

Beth: Last week, I was in Argentina on a hiking holiday and next week I'm going camping with a group of Spanish people.

Bob: What's your favourite country?

Beth: That's a difficult question. I like all the countries I visit. I prefer mountains and sea to cities, but they are all interesting.

Bob: How much do you see your husband?

Beth: I work in different countries a lot, but I work in different countries for one or two months and then I have one month at home. That's ok.

Bob: Ok. Now I'd like to ask some different questions. What can we do to help the environment?

Beth: Ha! ... Lots! But in my job I've got to go by plane. I don't like the pollution from planes, but I love my job. What can I do?

Bob: Good question! When you are at home, what do you do?

Beth: When I'm at home, I always walk to the village shop and the post office. My husband's got a car, but I never use it. My husband sometimes takes it to the market. And I've got a big recycling box in the garden. I recycle paper, bottles .... Every day I do something.

Bob: Thank, you Beth. That's very interesting.

1 Beth is ...
  a a pilot.
  b a tour guide.
  c an artist.

3 Beth is ...
  a Spanish.
  b married.
  c difficult.

5 Beth has got ...
  a a recycling box.
  b a bicycle.
  c a car.

2 Beth is going ...
  a to visit Argentina.
  b hiking.
  c camping.

4 Beth doesn't like ...
  a pollution.
  b flying.
  c difficult.

Score: ___ /5

© Pearson Education Limited 2018 PHOTOCOPIABLE

1 **Read. Then complete. (6 points)** (behind   expensive   heavy   pitch   sushi   thrillers)

1 I can _____ a tent. Look! I've put the pegs in.

2 How _____ is the elephant? It's 5,400 kilogrammes.

3 The shopping centre is _____ the theatre.

4 I made _____ yesterday. It was delicious!

5 I don't like _____. I prefer comedies.

6 My dad's new telescope was _____. It cost £300.

2 **Read and complete the questions. Then answer for you. (12 points)**

1 _____ (ever be) to a pop concert?   _____.

2 _____ (ever collect) rubbish?   _____.

3 _____ (ever play) the drums?   _____.

4 _____ (ever eat) paella?   _____.

5 _____ (see) the news today?   _____.

6 _____ (ever write) a story in English?   _____.

3 **Put the words in order to make sentences. (4 points)**

1 a / lighting / so / cold / I'm / fire / I'm

_____.

2 shopping / the / you / to / do / centre / how / get

_____?

3 new / you / her / song / have / yet / heard

_____?

4 if / paper / recycle / save / trees / you / you'll

_____.

4 **Describe the best film you've seen or the best game you've played. (8 points)**

• What was the name of film/game?   • What was the film about?/How do you play the game?

• What was the best part of the film/game?

_____

_____

_____

_____

_____

Score: ____ /30

Listen. Then circle. (8 points)

I'm going to the ¹(mountains / hills) next weekend. I can't wait! I'm going ²(camping / hiking) with my aunt and uncle. They go every weekend. I'm taking my green and purple ³(rucksack / torch) and a ⁴(compass / map). I learnt to read a compass last summer. I'll put my new ⁵(sleeping bag / bed) in the rucksack. My uncle is taking the ⁶(pegs / tent) and my aunt is taking the sleeping bags. We're going to make a ⁷(mess / campfire) and cook on the fire. My favourite camp food is ⁸(chips / rice) and beans.

 Listen. Then tick (✓). (5 points)

	rhino	camel	cheetah	whale	turtle
Hilary					
Pete					

Listen and complete. (7 points)

but   easier   complicated   interesting   more   scary   most

1 Engineering is more _____ than History. You need to know Maths.

2 Theme parks are more exciting than computer games, but they can be _____.

3 Music is _____ than Geography, and I like the Music teacher more.

4 I want to buy the _____ complicated telescope, but it's too expensive.

5 Riding a horse is more difficult than riding a bike, and it's _____ expensive.

6 Reading a book can be more _____ than watching a film, but it takes longer.

7 A house is more expensive than a car, _____ some cars are very expensive.

 Listen. Then number. (5 points)

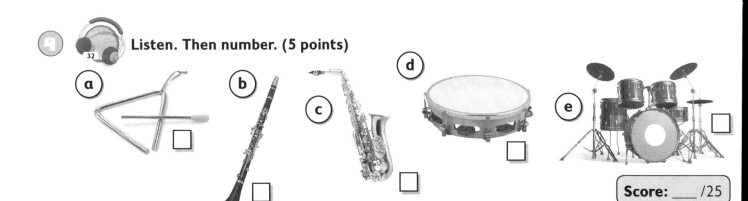

Score: ____ /25

1 Find 5 differences.

Score: ___ /5

Whole test score: ___ /65

1 Read. Then circle. (5 points)

Chris – the gardener

This month, I am going to talk to some people about their jobs. I want to find out where they live, what they like about their job and a little more information about their lives. This is Chris. Chris is a gardener. He works in a rural area in the south of England.

Bob: What do you like about your job, Chris?

Chris: I love being outside. I like sunny days and rainy days and I like stormy days.

Bob: Do you like snowy days?

Chris: Yes, I do, but not for gardening! It's a little cold in winter and there aren't many vegetables and flowers in the garden. In the winter, I usually tidy the garden and put out food for the birds when the snow comes and I often make little houses for other animals to hide in when it gets very cold.

Bob: What happens to the food you grow?

Chris: My wife and I usually cook the vegetables I grow. I've got potatoes and cabbages in my garden this year. Then I make jam from the fruit I've grown. I often sell the jam at the farmer's market. It tastes good and a lot of people in the village want more!

Bob: Is your wife a gardener?

Chris: She loves helping me in the garden, but she's a tour guide and is often on trips.

Bob: Ok. Now I'd like to ask some different questions. What should we do to help the environment?

Chris: Ha! ... Lots! I've got a small wildlife garden and I get lots of insects and birds there. I help to protect our wildlife and I help collect rubbish in our road. Some people just throw paper and rubbish everywhere. I feel sad for the animals that eat the rubbish and get ill and it doesn't look very nice.

Bob: Do you have a car?

Chris: Yes, I do. I take the car when I go shopping because the shopping is often very heavy. I go everywhere else by bicycle or on foot. It's better for the environment and better for my health!

Bob: Thank you Chris. That's very interesting.

1 Chris is …
  a a gardener.
  b a tour guide.
  c a singer.

2 In snowy weather, Chris …
  a makes jam.
  b rides his bicycle.
  c puts out food for the birds.

3 Chris is …
  a hungry.
  b married.
  c a farmer.

4 Chris has got a …
  a wildlife garden.
  b tidy garden.
  c small garden.

5 When Chris is shopping …
  a he goes by bicycle
  b he goes by car.
  c he walks.

Score: ___ /5

1 **Read. Then complete. (6 points)** ⟨ comedies   complicated   curry   light   tall   turn ⟩

1 It's cold on this campsite. Shall we _____ a fire?

2 How _____ is the giraffe? It's 5 metres.

3 _____ left and it's at the end of the road.

4 I made _____ yesterday. It was very hot!

5 I like watching _____. They make me laugh.

6 I want to use this app but it's very _____.

2 **Read and complete the questions. Then answer for you. (12 points)**

1 _____ (ever play) an instrument?   _____.

2 _____ (ever see) an alien?   _____.

3 _____ (ever eat) sushi?   _____.

4 _____ (ever be) to an aquarium?   _____.

5 _____ (hear) the news today?   _____.

6 _____ (ever read) a book in English?   _____.

3 **Put the words in order to make sentences. (4 points)**

1 bed / I'm / going / to / so / tired / I'm

_____.

2 sci-fi / you / yet / the / seen / film / have / new

_____?

3 ahead / left / go / straight / then / turn

_____.

4 if / bottles / recycle / reduce / waste / you / you'll

_____.

4 **Describe a good day. (8 points)**

- When was it?
- Who was there?
- Why was it good?
- What were they doing?
- What happened?

_____

_____

_____

_____

_____

Score: ___ /30

  Listen. Then complete. (8 points)

> camping   compass   cook   mountains
> rice   rucksack   sleeping bag   tent

I'm going to the ¹_____ next weekend. I can't wait! I'm going ²_____

with my aunt and uncle. They go every weekend. I'm taking my green and purple ³_____

and a ⁴_____. I learnt to read a compass last summer. I'll put my new ⁵_____

in the rucksack. My uncle is taking the ⁶_____ and my aunt is taking the sleeping bags.

We're going to make a campfire and ⁷_____ on the fire.

My favourite camp food is ⁸_____ and beans.

  Listen. Then write *T = True* or *F = False*. (5 points)

1 Hilary has seen a rhino. ☐   **2** Hilary has seen a camel. ☐

3 Hilary has seen a turtle. ☐   **4** Pete has seen a camel. ☐

5 Pete has seen a whale. ☐

  Listen and circle. (7 points)

1 Engineering is more (complicated / interesting) than History. You need to know Maths.

2 Theme parks are (less / more) exciting than computer games, but they can be scary.

3 Music is easier than (Geography / Science), and I like the Music teacher more.

4 I want to buy the (most / more) complicated telescope, but it's too expensive.

5 Riding a horse is more difficult than riding a bike, (and / but) it's more expensive.

6 Reading a book can be more (boring / interesting) than watching a film, but it takes longer.

7 A (house / horse) is more expensive than a car, but some cars are very expensive.

Listen. Then match. (5 points)

1 Owen   **2** Stuart   **3** Paul   **4** Ben   **5** Michelle

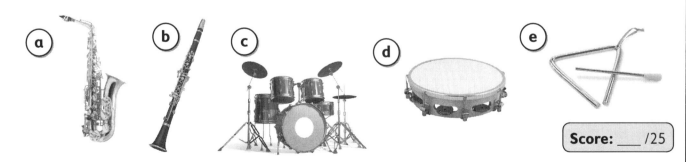

Score: ____ /25

1 Find 5 differences. (5 points)

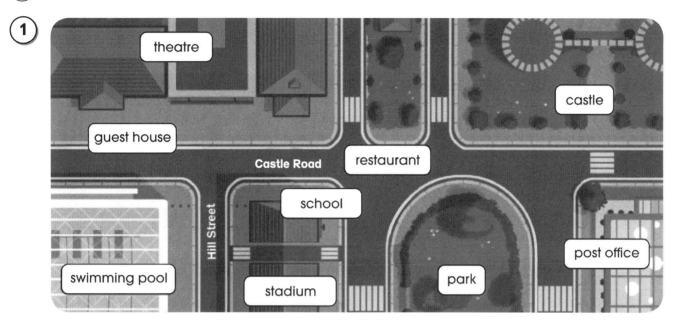

Score: ____ /5

Whole test score: ____ /65

1 **Look and read. Then choose the correct words. (6 points)**

> pegs   a whale   a cheetah   an airport   spaghetti   a telescope

1 This animal can run the fastest.   _____

2 You need this to look at the stars.   _____

3 You get planes from here.   _____

4 This is the biggest animal in the sea.   _____

5 You need these to pitch a tent.   _____

6 This is Italian food.   _____

2 **Look at the pictures. Write about this story. Write 20 or more words. (9 points)**

- Who are they, where are they?
- What are they doing?

- What can they see?
- What are they going to do?

_____

_____

_____

_____

_____

_____

_____

_____

_____

Score: ____ /15

3 Fiona is talking to her friend Charlotte. What does Charlotte say?
Write a letter (A–D) for each answer. (4 points)

1 **Fiona:**   Hi, Charlotte. What are you going to do tomorrow?

   Charlotte: ☐

2 **Fiona:**   What are you going to do there?

   Charlotte: ☐

3 **Fiona:**   Is your mum going?

   Charlotte: ☐

4 **Fiona:**   Where are you going?

   Charlotte: ☐

A   We're going to Italy.

B   I'm going to go on the boating lake.

C   No, she's going to the airport to get tickets for our holiday.

D   I'm going to go to the water park with my dad.

---

4 Read. Then complete. (10 points)

| aliens | amazing | astronaut | Earth | planets | rocket |
| satellites | stars | telescope | weather | | |

SUN

In space, there are lots of ¹_____ and ²_____. We can see them better if we've

got a ³_____. There are some ⁴_____ that go round the ⁵_____.

Some of them give us information about the ⁶_____. When I'm older, I'm going to be an

⁷_____. I want to travel in a ⁸_____. I'm going to look for ⁹_____.

Space is ¹⁰_____!

Score: ____ /14

Listen and draw lines. (6 points)

1 Ben **2** Jessica **3** Frank **4** Pam **5** Fiona **6** Trevor

  Listen. Then write. (6 points)

Holiday questionnaire	
Name:	
Class:	
Who went:	
Places visited:	
Animals seen:	
Favourite activity:	

Score: ____ /12

© Pearson Education Limited 2018   PHOTOCOPIABLE

3 **What are the children going to take on their camping holiday?**
Listen and draw lines. (4 points)

① Chris   **②** Joanna   **③** Martin   **④** Annabel

a    **b**    **c**    **d**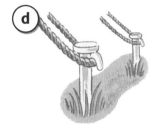

4 **Listen. Then tick (✓) the box. (9 points)**

1 What didn't Zoe see at the wildlife park?

a    **b**    **c**

2 What did Vicky do to help the environment?

a    **b**    **c**

3 Where is Fiona going?

a    **b**    **c**

Score: ____ /13

5 **Listen. Then colour and write. (5 points)**

Score: ____ /5

1 Look and read. Then choose the correct words. (6 points)

an alien   comedy   pollution   sushi   a tent   a railway station

1 You sleep in this when you are camping. _____

2 This doesn't help protect the planet. _____

3 Someone or something from a different planet. _____

4 A film which makes you laugh. _____

5 This is Japanese food. _____

6 You get trains from here. _____

2 Look at the pictures. Write about this story. Write 20 or more words. (9 points)

- Who are they, where are they?
- What are they doing?

- What can they see?
- What are they going to do?

_____
_____
_____
_____
_____
_____
_____
_____

Score: ___ /15

3 **Henry is talking to his friend Billy. What does Billy say?**
Write a letter (A–D) for each answer. (4 points)

1 **Henry:** Hi, Billy. What happened to you yesterday?

   Billy: ☐

2 **Henry:** Oh, no! Did you miss the Maths test?

   Billy: ☐

3 **Henry:** Was Mr Grant horrible?

   Billy: ☐

4 **Henry:** He wasn't angry? Wow! That was an important test!

   Billy: ☐

> **A** Yes, I did. I was too late!
>
> **B** I know. He gave me the test to do for homework.
>
> **C** No, he wasn't. He was amazing!
>
> **D** I missed the bus.

4 **Read. Then complete. (10 points)**

> amazing   biggest   camping
> fire   hiking   mountains   park
> pitch   railway station   read

I love ^{1}_____ and sleeping outside. We're going on a camping trip next week.

We're taking a train from the ^{2}_____. First I'm going to ^{3}_____ the tent then

I'm going to light a ^{4}_____. We're staying in a national ^{5}_____. We've been

there before. We will go ^{6}_____ in the ^{7}_____ and look at the wildlife.

I love animals. The ^{8}_____ animal I've seen is an elephant, but it was in the zoo.

I'm going with my mum. She loves camping and can ^{9}_____ a compass,

and answer my questions about animals. I think she's ^{10}_____!

Score: ____ /14

Listen and draw lines. (6 points)

1 Ben **2** Jessica **3** Frank **4** Pam **5** Fiona **6** Trevor

  Listen. Then correct the mistakes. (6 points)

Holiday questionnaire	
Name:	Sameera
Class:	9G
Who went:	mum and two brothers
Places visited:	a castle and an aquarium
Animals seen:	camel, cheetah and otter
Favourite activity:	going on the big wheel

Score: ____ /12

3 What are the children going to take on their camping holiday?
Listen and draw lines. **(4 points)**

1 Chris   **2** Joanna   **3** Martin   **4** Annabel

a    **b** 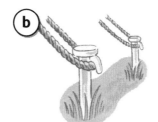   **c**    **d**

  4 Listen. Then tick (✓) the box. **(9 points)**

1 What didn't Zoe see at the wildlife park?

a    **b**    **c**

2 What did Vicky do to help the environment?

a    **b**    **c**

3 Where is Fiona going?

a   **b**    **c**

Score: ____ /13

5 **Listen. Then colour and write. (5 points)**

Score: ___ /5

1 Ask your teacher questions. Then complete. (10 points)

	Gemma's brother
Name	
Age	
Colour of eyes	
Favourite food	
Likes	

	Jack's sister
Name	
Age	
Colour of eyes	
Favourite food	
Likes	

2 Look at the pictures. Then tell a story. (10 points)

a

b

c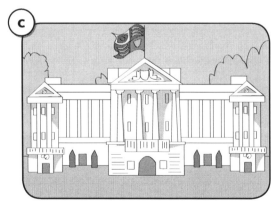

d

Score: ____ /20

3 **Choose a topic you know about. Draw a mind map. Then talk. (10 points)**

- Where you live.
- Help to protect your planet.
- Wildlife.
- Your last summer trip.

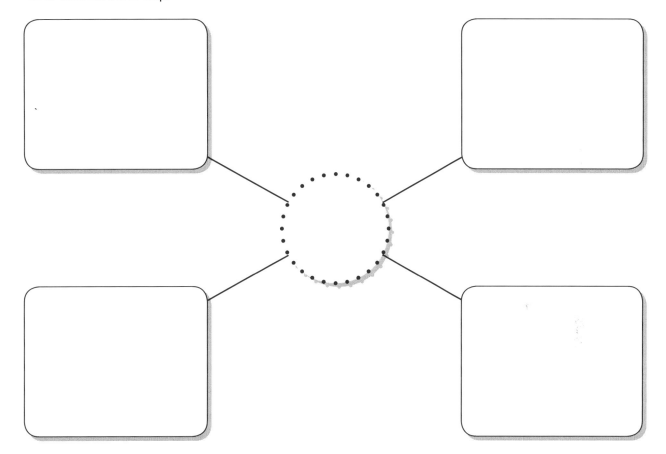

4 **Ask and answer questions. (10 points)**

- Is it important to protect the planet? Why?
- What should we do to protect the planet?
- Should schools teach us how to protect the planet?
- What things do you do to protect the planet?

Score: ____ /20

Placement

Reading

1   **1** were – b   **2** these – g   **3** much – e   **4** is – f
   5 When – h   **6** Was – d   **7** taller – a   **8** on – c

2   **1** f   **2** e   **3** b   **4** a   **5** c   **6** d

3   **1** T   **2** T   **3** F   **4** F   **5** T   **6** T

Writing

1   **1** What's he like?
   2 What's she good at?
   3 What did you do yesterday?
   4 What are you going to buy?
   5 What were you doing yesterday evening?
   6 How often do you go running?

2   **1** Ellie is good at sports.
   2 The ball was in the playground.
   3 I played tennis with my friends.
   4 I was walking the dog yesterday.
   5 It's an American film which is very famous.

3   (open answers)

Listening and speaking

1   **1** uncle   **2** tomorrow   **3** next week   **4** camping
   5 quickly   **6** hiking   **7** boat   **8** Brazil   **9** very
   10 birds   **11** saw

2   **1** 4 o'clock – c   **2** were – f   **3** Harry – e
   4 What's – d   **5** notes in class – a   **6** Did – b

3   (suggested questions and answers) What are these boys doing? (They're throwing and catching a ball). What are these girls doing? (They're playing tennis.) What is this girl doing? (She's walking a dog.) What does the girl who is kicking a ball look like? (She's got long dark hair. She's smiling. She's wearing shorts and a T-shirt.)

Unit 1

Reading and writing A

1   **1** torch – d   **2** campsite – e   **3** tent – a   **4** compass – b
   5 fire – c

2   **1** b   **2** e   **3** f   **4** a   **5** d   **6** c

3   **1** camping   **2** tents   **3** put   **4** sleeping bags   **5** lighting
   6 fire   **7** compass

4   (open answers)

Listening and speaking A

1   **1** T   **2** F   **3** T   **4** F   **5** F

2   **1** can   **2** read a compass   **3** light a fire   **4** sleeping bag

3   (example answers) They are (camping). They're (pitching a tent). He's (cooking). She's (putting in the pegs). She's (reading a compass). The dog (is digging a hole under the boys' tent). I love (camping). He/She loves (camping in the mountains).

Reading and writing B

1   **1** peg(s) – b   **2** sleeping bag – e   **3** rucksack – c
   4 torch – d   **5** compass – a

2   **1** pitching the tent
   2 covering their heads
   3 setting up the bed
   4 keeping out of the rain
   5 putting in the pegs
   6 reading the compass

3   **1** campsite   **2** tents   **3** pitch   **4** putting in
   5 setting up   **6** lighting   **7** compass

4   (open answers)

Listening and speaking B

1   **1** family   **2** is   **3** like   **4** older   **5** are

2   **1** T   **2** F   **3** T   **4** T

3   (example answers) They are (camping). They're (pitching a tent). He's (cooking). She's (putting in the pegs). She's (reading a compass). The dog (is digging a hole under the boys' tent). I love (camping). He/She loves (camping in the mountains).

Unit 2

Reading and writing A

1   **1** rhino – d   **2** cheetah – b   **3** koala – f   **4** lemur – c
   5 camel – e   **6** whale – a

2   **1** How heavy is a rhino? – c   **2** How tall is a giraffe? – a
   3 Are cheetahs more dangerous than lemurs? – d
   4 Which is the longest? – b

3   **1** The giraffe is the tallest.
   2 The snake is the longest.
   3 The turtle is the slowest.
   4 The butterfly is the lightest.

4   (open answers)

Listening and speaking A

1   a 3   b 8   c 7   d 2   e 1   f 4   g 5   h 6

2   **1** bigger – c   **2** heaviest – f   **3** tiger – a   **4** seals – b
   5 smallest – e   **6** fast – d

3   (example answers) The turtle is (the lightest). The rhino is (the heaviest). The whale is (the biggest). The giraffe is (the tallest). The cheetah is (the fastest). The turtle is (1.6 metres long). The rhino is (1,600 kilogrammes). The giraffe is (five metres tall). The cheetah is (1.1 to 1.5 metres long). The (blue) whale is (140,000 kilogrammes).

Reading and writing B

1   **1** seal – d   **2** tiger – f   **3** otter – a   **4** turtle – b
   5 rhino – c   **6** koala– e

2   **1** How long is an elephant? – c
   2 How heavy is a cheetah? – d
   3 Are tigers more dangerous than turtles? – a
   4 Which is the heaviest? – b

3 1 the ant is the smallest.
2 The cheetah is the fastest.
3 The whale is the biggest.
4 The butterfly is the lightest.

4 (open answers)

Listening and speaking B

1 a 4   b 6   c 5   d 7   e 8   f 2   g 3   h 1

2 1 bigger – f   2 heaviest – a   3 tiger – b   4 seals – c
5 smallest – d   6 fast – e

3 (example answers) (The cheetahs) are the fastest. (The rhinos) are the biggest. (The hippo) is the heaviest. (The butterfly) is the smallest. (Cheetahs) are found in (Africa). (Tigers) are rescued in (India). (Lemurs) are seen in (Africa/Madagascar).

Unit 3
Reading and writing A

1 1 station   2 straight   3 end   4 in   5 house   6 first

2 1 shopping centre   2 swimming pool   3 Turn left out of the house. Walk/Go straight ahead. At the end of the road, turn left. It's the second building on the left.
4 Turn right out of the college. Go straight ahead and turn right into Green Road. Go to the end of the road and turn right. Take the first road on the right.

Listening and speaking A

1 1 b   2 b   3 a   4 a   5 c

2 1 we   2 cinema   3 should   4 circus   5 finish

3 (example answers) Is there (a theatre)? Are there (any restaurants)? How do you get to the (supermarket)? If you (turn left, you will find the park opposite the supermarket). It's on the corner of (Station Road and Hill Street)/at the end of (Station Road)/ in front of (the park)

Reading and writing B

1 1 office   2 ahead   3 front   4 road   5 stop   6 second

2 1 cinema   2 swimming pool   3 Turn left into Park Road and then turn right into Green Road. Go straight ahead to the end of the road and turn right into Station Road. It's the second building on the left.   4 Turn right into Station Road and take the first left into Green Road. Go straight ahead and at the end of the road turn left. Go down Park Road. It's the third building on the left.

Listening and speaking B

1 1 e   2 a   3 d   4 c   5 b

2 1 park   2 cinema   3 chemist's   4 we   5 can

3 (example answers) Is there (a theatre)? Are there (any restaurants)? How do you get to the (supermarket)? If you (turn left, you can find the park opposite the supermarket). It's on the corner of (Station Road and Hill Street)/at the end of (Station Road)/ in front of (the park)

Unit 4
Reading and writing A

1 1 made   2 food   3 read   4 turned   5 had   6 dishes

2 1 F   2 T   3 F   4 T   5 F   6 T

3 1 They watched two films and played computer games.
2 Because she loves chicken.   3 Caroline/She helped Tina's dad.   4 Because Caroline ate it.

4 1 She made a list.   2 She bought food.
3 She washed the dishes.   4 She served a meal.

Listening and speaking A

1 Tom: beans, cheese, chips, spaghetti
Sarah: banana, chicken, rice, salad

2 1 F   2 T   3 T   4 F   5 F   6 F

3 (example answers) I (went to the park and played football). I (saw my friend). I didn't (do homework). It made me (happy).

Reading and writing B

1 1 list   2 recipe   3 prepared   4 oven   5 had   6 washed

2 1 d   2 b   3 e   4 a   5 f   6 c

3 1 Yes, he was.   2 Because he swam for two hours.
3 They had chicken curry and rice. They played with George's computer.

4 1 She made a list.   2 She read a recipe.
3 She prepared ingredients.   4 They had a meal.

Listening and speaking B

1 1 spaghetti   2 cheese   3 chips   4 beans   5 chicken
6 rice   7 cake   8 banana

2 1 ✓   2 ✗   3 ✗   4 ✓   5 ✓   6 ✗

3 (example answers) I went (to the shop). I forgot (the list). I didn't (serve a cake because I didn't turn on the oven). It made me (sad).

Unit 5
Reading and writing A

1 1 thriller   2 sci-fi   3 comedy   4 fantasy

2 1 played the cello/violin? Yes, I have./No, I haven't.
2 been to a musical? Yes, I have./No, I haven't.
3 played the harmonica? Yes, I have./No, I haven't.
4 listened to the harp? Yes, I have./No, I haven't.

3 1 F   2 T   3 F   4 F

4 1 hasn't done   2 has never made   3 have lived
4 have already seen

Listening and speaking A

1 1 played   2 listened   3 found   4 seen   5 bought
6 played

2 1 T   2 F   3 T   4 T   5 T   6 F   7 T   8 F

3 (example answers) The band are playing (rock music). There are two men (playing the guitar) and a man (playing the drums). One man (is singing). There are (two guitars) and (four drums).

Reading and writing B

1   **1** musical   **2** cartoon   **3** romance   **4** biography

2   **1** Have you ever seen a thriller? Yes, I have./No, I haven't.
    2 Have you ever played the tambourine? Yes, I have./No, I haven't.
    3 How long have you lived in your house? I have lived in my house for (ten years)/since (2010).
    4 Have you ever drawn a cartoon? Yes, I have./No, I haven't.

3   **1** F   **2** T   **3** F   **4** T

4   **1** has lived   **2** has never eaten   **3** haven't done
    4 have already made

Listening and speaking B

1   **1** T   **2** F   **3** F   **4** T   **5** T   **6** F

2   **1** piano   **2** classical   **3** cello   **4** harmonica
    5 saxophones   **6** drums   **7** tambourine   **8** triangle

3   (example answers) The concert was (at the football stadium/arena). I heard (saxophones and guitars and drums). I have never (played the drums). I have played (the tambourine).

Unit 6

Reading and writing A

1   **1** d   **2** a   **3** c   **4** b

2   **1** I'm not sure. It's very expensive. – 2
    2 That's a good idea! – 5
    3 We could go to the palace. – 4
    4 What else could we do? – 3

3   **1** Sally/She's going to go to a theme park.
    2 She'll go on the pirate ship first.
    3 After lunch, she'll go on the boating lake.
    4 She could go on the big wheel.

4   (suggested answers)   **1** Shall we go to the.
    2 I don't like hiking.   **3** What else could we do?
    4 That's a good idea.

Listening and speaking A

1   **1** T   **2** F   **3** F   **4** T   **5** T

2   **1** big wheel   **2** rollercoaster   **3** boating lake
    4 dodgems   **5** pirate ship   **6** mini golf

3   (example answers) I will stay (in a hotel by the beach). The weather will be (sunny). I will (go swimming in the sea). I will get there (by plane). I will take (my swimming costume).

Reading and writing B

1   **1** a   **2** d   **3** b   **4** c

2   **1** Shall we go hiking in the National Park? – c
    2 I'm not sure. – b
    3 No, I went last weekend. – a
    4 We could go to the castle. – d

3   **1** He's got a lot of work to do.
    2 She loves studying dinosaurs.
    3 After the dinosaurs, she'll see the fossils.
    4 (If Gemma/she has time,) she will go to the theatre.

4   (suggested answers)
    1 Shall we go to the [name of place]?
    2 Shall we go hiking (in the National Park)?
    3 We could go to the [name of place].   **4** Let's do that.

Listening and speaking B

1   **1** ✗   **2** ✗   **3** ✓   **4** ✗   **5** ✓

2   **a** 4   **b** 5   **c** 1   **d** 3   **e** 2   **f** 6

3   (example answers) I will stay (in a hotel). It will be (snowing/snowy). I will (go snowboarding). I will get there (by car). I will take (my ski goggles).

Unit 7

Reading and writing A

1   **1** Astronauts need to do exercise in space.
    2 You shouldn't look directly at the sun.
    3 You had better do your homework tonight.
    4 Joe needs to find out about Mars for his project.
    5 You ought to tidy your bedroom.
    6 We should watch that film about aliens.

2   **1** F   **2** F   **3** F   **4** T   **5** T   **6** F

3   (open answers)

Listening and speaking A

1   **1** T   **2** F   **3** F   **4** T   **5** F   **6** T   **7** F

2   **1** story   **2** journey   **3** telescope   **4** photograph   **5** film
    6 astronaut

3   (example answers) It's (small and is a circle shape). It (has got spots on it). It's not (very complicated). It's (interesting/amazing). (Small green aliens) live there.

Teacher to guess which picture.

Reading and writing B

1   **1** You had better tidy your bedroom after dinner.
    2 We ought to call the police.
    3 Harry should listen to the teacher.
    4 We need to write about astronauts for our homework.
    5 I ought to visit my grandparents.
    6 Dad doesn't need to take his telescope.

2   **1** It's Jackie's dad's telescope.
    2 It's big and very complicated.
    3 (Jackie/She can see) stars and planets and comets.
    4 Jackie's dad/He is brilliant/very clever/intelligent.
    5 Jackie/She should put a coat/jacket/boots on.
    6 The best way (to learn about space) is looking at the stars./Looking at the stars is the best way (to learn about space).

3   (open answers)

Listening and speaking B

1   **1** planets   **2** telescope   **3** alien   **4** astronaut   **5** rocket
    6 spaceship   **7** comets

2   **1** d   **2** f   **3** a   **4** c   **5** e   **6** b

3   (example answers) It's a (big). It has got (ten boosters). It's (interesting/complicated/amazing). (Six astronauts) live there.

Teacher to guess which picture.

Unit 8
Reading and writing A
1 1 d   2 c   3 a   4 b

2 1 collect rubbish – a   2 turn lights off – c
3 reuse plastic bags – e   4 use public transport – b
5 recycle paper – d

3 1 T   2 T   3 F   4 T   5 T   6 F

Listening and speaking A
1 a 4   b 5   c 3   d 6   e 1   f 2

2 1 F   2 T   3 F   4 T   5 T   6 T

3 (example answers) I always/sometimes/often (recycle paper) because (I want to save trees). If I (recycle bottles, I will help save resources). If I don't (turn off the lights, my parents won't be happy). I can (reuse plastic bags). I can't (take the bottles to the recycling bins).

Reading and writing B
1 1 c   2 d   3 a   4 b

2 1 b E   2 d A   3 e C   4 a D   5 c B

3 1 (you should) put it in the bin.
2 (We can) use public transport.
3 (We can keep plastic bags) in our bag or in the car.
4 We conserve energy.
5 We can recycle bottles.
6 We can recycle paper.

Listening and speaking B
1 1 T   2 F   3 F   4 T   5 F   6 T

2 1 b   2 f   3 d   4 e   5 a   6 c

3 (example answers) I (recycle paper because I want to save trees). If we (collect rubbish, we will keep the planet clean). If we don't (use public transport, we won't reduce pollution). I can (turn off the lights). I can't (use public transport because there are no buses to my village).

End of term 1
Reading and writing
1 1 d   2 f   3 a   4 e   5 g   6 b   7 c

2 1 a   2 e   3 d   4 c   5 f   6 b

3 1 going, don't   2 putting   3 doing, pitching   4 dancing
5 heaviest   6 tallest   7 want, go

4 1 camping   2 pitched   3 put in   4 fire   5 sang
6 saw   7 taller   8 heaviest   9 fossils   10 between
11 cinema

5 1 Go straight ahead and turn right. Go straight ahead and it's at the end of London Road. It's near/in front of the college.
2 Go straight ahead and turn left. Go straight ahead. It's on the right, next to/behind the sports centre.
3 Go straight ahead and turn right. Go to the end of London Road. It's on the right, near the factory/between the factory and shopping centre.

Listening and speaking
1 1 eight   2 camping   3 pegs   4 lighting   5 down
6 campsite   7 sea   8 ten   9 hiking   10 sailing

---

11 river   12 raining   13 rain   14 tent   15 pitch
16 climbing   17 rucksack   18 sleeping bag   19 torch
20 campsite

2 1 650   2 804   3 313   4 5/five   5 2½/two and a half

3 1 a 5   b 6   c 2   d 3   e 4   f 1
2 a 2   b 6   c 4   d 3   e 5   f 1

4 (example answers) It's a (rhino). It's (one and a half) metres long. It's (five hundred) kilogrammes. The (tiger) is taller than the (otter). The (rhino) is heavier than the (cheetah). The (rhino) is the tallest animal. The (rhino) is the heaviest animal.

End of term 2
Reading and writing
1 1 b   2 d   3 h   4 f   5 a   6 c   7 e   8 g

2 1 f   2 b   3 a   4 d   5 c   6 e

3 (open answers)

4 music: jazz, country, blues, rock, pop
films: thriller, musical, cartoon, romance, sci-fi, comedy
a thriller   b comedy   c blues   d cartoon   e rock
f jazz   g pop   h musical   i romance   j sci-fi   k country

5 (open answers)

Listening and speaking
1 a 3   b 5   c 1   d 4   e 6   f 2

2 1 ill   2 was playing   3 was   4 has been   5 Ellie
6 books   7 he wasn't hungry

3 1 f   2 c   3 a   4 b   5 e   6 d

4 (example answers. Teacher to respond and spell if required.)
1 What is the name of the restaurant? *(It's) Paella City*
What type of food can you eat there? *(You can eat) Spanish paella.*
Who eats there? *The Hart family (eat there).*
Where is the restaurant? *(It's on) London Road.*
How many stars has it got? *(It's got) four stars.*

2 What is the name of the restaurant? *(It's) Curry World.*
What type of food can you eat there? *(You can eat) hot curries!*
Who eats there? *The Ball family (eat there).*
Where is the restaurant? *(It's) in the square.*
How many stars has it got? *(It's got) five stars.*

5 (example answers) A good day: (I met my friend Mike). I went to (the park). I played (football with Mike). I ate (fish and chips). It was a good day because (I had fun). A bad day: (I had an accident). I went to (my grandma's house). I dropped (my plate of pasta). I didn't eat (pasta). It was a bad day because (I had an accident).

End of term 3
Reading and writing
1 1 Which   2 ought   3 most   4 you   5 What, rubbish
6 going, recycle

2 1 The comet is more interesting than the planet – c
2 The big telescope is more complicated than the small telescope – f

---

3 I am going to recycle some bottles – d
4 She's going to recycle some paper – a
5 They are going to use public transport – e
6 The green alien is more/less frightening than the yellow alien – b

3 **1** You should wear a hat because it's cold.
2 We had better go inside.
3 They ought to look at the stars.
4 The white spaceship is the most amazing.
5 The astronomer is very interesting.
6 One hot day we decided to go swimming./We decided to go swimming one hot day.

4 **1** d **2** e **3** a **4** b **5** f **6** c

5 (open answers)

Listening and speaking

1 **1** alien **2** intelligent **3** planets **4** frightening
5 complicated **6** haven't **7** aliens **8** doesn't tell

2 ✓ collect rubbish, use public transport, recycle paper, recycle bottles

3 **1** Tereshkova **2** Vostok 6 **3** 16th June **4** three/3
5 48

4 (example answers. Teacher to respond and spell if required.)
1 What is the name of the astronaut? *(It's) Tim Saturn.*
Where did he go? *(He went to) Jupiter.*
What's the name of the/his rocket? *(It's/It's name is Apollo 600.*
What did he see? *(He saw) 96 moons.*
When did he go (there/to Jupiter)? *He went (there/to Jupiter) on the 21st (of) March.*
2 What is the name of the astronaut? *(It's) Astrid Mars.*
Where did she go? *(She went to) the Moon.*
What's the name of the/her rocket? *(It's/It's name is Challenger 99.*
What did she see? *(She saw) volcanoes.*
When did she go (there/to the Moon)? *She went (there/to the Moon) on the 10th (of) December.*

5 (example answers) I can recycle (paper/bottles). I can use (public transport). I can collect (rubbish). I can reuse (plastic bags). I can take (a shower).

6 (example answers. Teacher to read text in speech bubble to prompt pupils)
1 *One day in April last year, a spaceship landed in a field. It was only four o'clock in the morning, but the noise and the lights woke Jake up. He looked out of his bedroom window.*
2 Jake put on his clothes and ran to the spaceship. Some strange men got out of the spaceship.
3 They had large heads and were green. 'Am I dreaming?' thought Jake.
4 'Welcome to our UFO,' said an alien. Jake screamed and tried to run away.
5 In the end, Jake woke up. It was time for school. It was only a dream.

Final test
Reading A
1 **1** b **2** c **3** b **4** a **5** a

Writing A
1 **1** pitch **2** heavy **3** behind **4** sushi **5** thrillers
6 expensive

2 **1** Have you ever been, Yes, I have./No, I haven't.
2 Have you ever collected, Yes, I have./No, I haven't.
3 Have you ever played, Yes, I have./No, I haven't.
4 Have you ever eaten, Yes, I have./No, I haven't.
5 Have you seen, Yes, I have./No, I haven't.
6 Have you ever written, Yes, I have./No, I haven't.

3 **1** I'm cold so I'm lighting a fire.
2 How do you get to the shopping centre?
3 Have you heard her new song yet?
4 If you recycle paper, you'll save trees./You'll save trees if you recycle paper.

4 (open answers)

Listening A
1 **1** mountains **2** camping **3** rucksack **4** compass
5 sleeping bag **6** tent **7** campfire **8** rice

2 Hilary: ✓ camel, whale, turtle
Pete: ✓ rhino, whale

3 **1** complicated **2** scary **3** easier **4** most **5** more
6 interesting **7** but

4 **1** e **2** c **3** a **4** d **5** b

Speaking A
1 (example answers) In the first picture the boy has got two white shoes. In the second picture the boy has got a black and a white shoe.
In the first picture the boy is standing on his right leg. In the second picture the boy is standing on his left leg.
In the first picture there are three stars. In the second picture there are four stars.
In the first picture the big aliens are standing next to each other. In the second picture the big aliens are standing on each side of a small alien.
In the first picture the smallest alien isn't smiling. In the second picture the smallest alien is smiling.

Reading B
1 **1** a **2** c **3** b **4** a **5** b

Writing B
1 **1** light **2** tall **3** Turn **4** curry **5** comedies
6 complicated

2 **1** Have you ever played, Yes, I have./No, I haven't.
2 Have you ever seen, Yes, I have./No, I haven't.
3 Have you ever eaten, Yes, I have./No, I haven't.
4 Have you ever been, Yes, I have./No, I haven't.
5 Have you heard, Yes, I have./No, I haven't.
6 Have you ever read, Yes, I have./No, I haven't.

3 **1** I'm tired so I'm going to bed.
2 Have you seen the new sci-fi film yet?
3 Turn left then go straight ahead./Go straight ahead then turn left.

4 If you recycle bottles, you'll reduce waste./You'll reduce waste if you recycle bottles.

4 (open answers)

Listening B

1 **1** mountains **2** camping **3** rucksack **4** compass
5 sleeping bag **6** tent **7** cook **8** rice

2 **1** F **2** T **3** T **4** F **5** T

3 **1** complicated **2** more **3** Geography **4** most **5** but
6 interesting **7** house

4 **1** c **2** a **3** e **4** d **5** b

Speaking B

1 (example answers) In the first picture the guest house is next to the theatre. In the second picture the guest house is next to the school.
In the first picture the school is next to the stadium. In the second picture the school is next to the guest house. In the first picture the stadium is in Hill Street. In the second picture the stadium is next to the park. In the first picture the post office is next to the park. In the second picture the post office is next to the theatre.
In the first picture the road is called Castle Road. In the second picture the road is called Station Road.

Exam preparation

Reading and writing A

1 **1** a cheetah **2** a telescope **3** an airport **4** a whale
5 pegs **6** spaghetti

2 (example answers) There are two aliens. They are on Earth. There is a lot of pollution. They will home to get more aliens to help collect rubbish and keep the planet clean.

3 **1** D **2** B **3** C **4** A

4 **1** planets/stars **2** stars/planets **3** telescope
4 satellites **5** Earth **6** weather **7** astronaut
8 rocket **9** aliens **10** amazing

Listening A

1 **1** b **2** c **3** f **4** d **5** a **6** e

2 **1** Samantha **2** 5T **3** mum and dad and two sisters
4 a wildlife park and a theme park
5 giraffe, tigers, lemur **6** going to the theme park

3 **1** c **2** b **3** a **4** d

4 **1** b **2** c **3** c

5 **1** telescope – red and brown
2 two stars closest to the planet – purple and blue
3 WELCOME TO SPACE – next to the astronaut
4 boy's space suit – yellow and orange
5 space suit of alien sitting and pressing buttons – pink and green

Reading and writing B

1 **1** a tent **2** pollution **3** an alien **4** comedy
5 sushi **6** a railway station

2 (example answers) There are two astronauts. They are fixing the spaceship. They can see Earth, but they are living on a space station. They will go to the space station to do some Science.

3 **1** D **2** A **3** C **4** B

4 **1** camping **2** railway station **3** pitch **4** fire
5 park **6** hiking **7** mountains **8** biggest **9** read
10 amazing

Listening B

1 **1** a **2** f **3** b **4** c **5** e **6** d

2 **1** Samantha **2** 5T **3** mum and dad and two sisters
4 a wildlife park and a theme park
5 giraffe, tigers, lemur **6** going to the theme park

3 **1** a **2** c **3** d **4** b

4 **1** a **2** b **3** a

5 **1** telescope – red and brown
2 two stars closest to the planet – purple and blue
3 WELCOME TO SPACE – next to the astronaut
4 boy's space suit – yellow and orange
5 space suit of alien sitting and pressing buttons – pink and green

Speaking A and B

1 (example answers. Teacher to respond and spell if required.)
What is Jack's sister's name? *Her name is Sandra.*
How old is she? *She's two.*
What colour are her eyes? *They're brown.*
What's her favourite food? *It's spaghetti.*
What does she like? *She likes crying and laughing.*
What is Gemma's brother's name? *His name is Ben.*
How old is he? *She's eleven.*
What colour are his eyes? *They're blue.*
What's his favourite food? *It's curry.*
What does he like? *He likes theme parks.*

2 **1** The boys are at the aquarium. They can see some fish.
2 Now they're at the Natural History museum. They can see some dinosaurs and paintings.
3 Now they're at the palace. They can see a big building.
4 Now they're at the water park. They're on the water slide. They're having fun.

3 I live in (name of town or city). There's a (water park) there. I (recycle paper) to protect my planet. I (reuse plastic bags). I (have seen an otter). I (have never seen a camel). I (went camping in the mountains last summer). We (lit a fire and sang songs).

4 Yes, it's important to protect the planet because (we only have one planet). Do you think it's important?

We should (recycle paper). We should (use public transport). Do you use public transport?

Schools should teach us how to protect the planet. Which lesson should teach us?

I (reuse plastic bags). I recycle (bottles). What do you do to protect the planet?

Audio files are available on the ActiveTeach, or at www.pearsonelt.com/catalogue/primary/poptropica-english-islands

M: Man

W: Woman

Placement

Placement test. Test Booklet. Activity 1. Listen. Then complete.

M: This is Andy. He's my uncle. He's a tour guide. He goes to a lot of different countries. Tomorrow he is going to Colombia and next week, he is going to China. Sometimes he takes groups camping. He likes camping. He can pitch a tent very quickly and can pitch it in the dark! Sometimes he takes a group hiking in the hills and mountains or on boat trips in Brazil.
Last year I went with him to Brazil. It was great. One day we went on a boat trip on the Amazon River. It was very foggy on the river when we got to the boat. But it was beautiful. From the boat we could hear the sounds of birds and monkeys in the trees. They were very noisy! And we saw some tapir drinking water from the river. It was amazing. I want to be a tour guide when I'm older!

Placement test. Test Booklet. Activity 2. Listen and circle. Then listen angain and match.

1

M: What were you doing yesterday at 4 o'clock, Sarah?

W: I was walking home from school.

2

W: What were you doing yesterday morning before school, Ed?

M: I was having my breakfast and finishing my homework for today!

3

M: What does Harry look like?

W: He's got short, blond hair and blue eyes.

4

M: What's Harry like?

W: He's sporty and hard-working.

5

W: Do you take notes in class?

M: Yes, I do.

6

W: Did you go to the party last weekend?

M: No, I couldn't. My grandparents were visiting.

Unit 1

Unit 1. Tests A and B. Test Booklet. Activity 1. Test A. Listen. Then write T = True or F = False. Test B. Listen. Then circle.

W: Hi, I'm Joanna. I'm on an adventure camp with my family. This is Will. He's my little brother. He loves adventure camps because he's really good at sports.
Mum and Dad love camping. They camp every weekend when the weather is sunny and they camp in the rain and snow, too!
My two older sisters, Sarah and Kim, are pitching their tent. At the moment, they're putting in the tent pegs.

Unit 1. Tests A and B. Test Booklet. Activity 2. Test A. Listen. Then circle. Test B. Listen. Then write T = True or F = False.

1

W: Will can't play football but he can pitch a tent. Camping is his favourite activity.

2

W: Joanna's mum can read a map and read a compass. She loves map reading.

3

W: Sarah and Kim can pitch and take down a tent but they can't make and light a campfire.

4

W: Oh no! Sonia is putting the sleeping bags in the tents and her sleeping bag isn't in her rucksack!

Unit 2

Unit 2. Tests A and B. Test Booklet. Activity 1. Listen. Then number in the correct order.

M1: Hey, Dad. This term at school, we're studying wild animals. We're finding out information about the different animals. I've also got to write some questions to ask my classmates. Listen. These are the questions. Number one: How heavy is a koala? Number two: How fast can a cheetah run?

M2: Slow down!! ... OK ... first there was a question about a koala? And then a question about a cheetah.

M1: Yes, exactly! And there are six more. Listen. Number three: Are whales the biggest animals? Number four: Are otters the lightest animals? Number five: How tall is a camel?

M2: Hah. Now you're asking questions about whales, otters and camels.

M1: Yes. Can I continue?

M2: Yes, of course.

M1: OK ... Number six is: How big is a lemur? And number seven is: Are white rhinos extinct? The last question is: Number eight: How heavy are the wings of a butterfly? So ... are they easy or difficult?

M2: Well ... I'd need to find out some of the answers on the internet ... but they're interesting questions. Ask your mum the questions!

Unit 2. Tests A and B. Test Booklet. Activity 2. Test A. Listen and circle. Then match. Test B. Listen and write. Then match.

1

M1: Are whales bigger than otters?

M2: Yes, they are.

2

W1: Which is the heaviest, the rhino or the turtle?

W2: Er ... the rhino ... but aren't there some giant turtles in South America?

3

M1: Ok ... Is the tiger the lightest animal?

M2: No, it isn't.

4

W1: And … Are seals taller than rhinos?

W2: No, they aren't.

5

M1: Right. So … Which is the smallest: the otter, the koala or the lemur?

M2: The lemur.

6

W1: How fast is the cheetah?

W2: Very fast!!

Unit 3
Unit 3. Tests A and B. Test Booklet. Activity 1. Test A. Listen. Then circle. Test B. Listen. Then match.

1

W1: Excuse me. How do I get to the supermarket?

W2: Go straight ahead on this road. Then take the second turning on the left and the supermarket is on the right, next to the swimming pool.

W1: Thank you.

2

W1: Excuse me. How do I get to the newsagent's?

W2: If you want to go to the newsagent's, turn right at the corner then go straight ahead, and it's on the left between the bookshop and the chemist.

W1: Thank you

3

M1: Excuse me. How do I get to the station?

M2: Go straight ahead … towards the river. Go over the bridge and the station is in front of you.

M1: Thank you.

4

W1: Where do you want to go?

M1: I want to go to the college. How do I get there?

W1: Take bus number 33 from this bus stop and get off at Green Street. The college is in front of the bus stop.

M1: Thanks.

5

M2: I want to go to the post office. How do I get there?

W1: If you want a post office you'll have to go into town. There isn't a post office near here.

Unit 3. Tests A and B. Test Booklet. Activity 2. Test A. Listen. Then complete. Test B. Listen and circle.

1

W: If the weather is good, we can go to the park.

2

W: I can go to the cinema if I'm not too tired.

3

W: If you're ill, you should go to the chemist's.

4

W: If you want to have fun, we can go to the circus.

5

W: If you finish your homework, you can come to the shopping centre.

Unit 4
Unit 4. Tests A and B. Test Booklet. Activity 1. Test A. Listen. Then tick (✓). Test B. Listen. Then complete.

M: What did you have for dinner last night, Sarah?

W: I had a big bowl of soup to start with. What about you Tom … What did you have?

M: I had some spaghetti and cheese to start with.

W: Then what did you have?

M: I had some chips and beans. What about you?

W: Mum cooked some Thai chicken and rice. It was lovely.

M: Did you have any biscuits or cake?

W: No. I had some salad and then I ate a banana.

M: Mmm. Too healthy! I ate a bag of sweets I bought after school.

Unit 4. Tests A and B. Test Booklet. Activity 2. Listen. Then write T = True or F = False.

W: Hi, I'm Debbie. Yesterday was a good day. It was my Dad's birthday so I made him a cake.
First, I got up early and made a list. Then I went to the shop and bought the ingredients. While I was walking home, I saw my friend. She said she wanted to help make the cake. My friend read the recipe and I prepared the ingredients. Then, when the mixture was ready, we turned on the oven and put the cake in. While we were washing the dishes, we listened to music. Dad came home and we served the cake and sang. He was very happy!

Unit 5
Unit 5. Tests A and B. Test Booklet. Activity 1. Test A. Listen and write. Test B. Listen. The write T = True or F = False.

1

W1: Have you ever played the harp, Christine?

W2: No, I haven't. I want to learn but it's very difficult.

2

M1: Steve, have your mum and dad listened to your brother playing the trumpet in a concert?

M2: Yes, they have. They always enjoy themselves.

3

W1: Karen, has your sister found the triangle?

W2: Yes, she has. Here it is.

4

M1: Have you seen my harmonica, Tom?

M2: No, I haven't. Is it in your school bag?

5

W1: Has Bob bought a saxophone?

W2: Yes, he has. He bought one last week.

6

M1: Have you ever played the drums, Ron?

M2: Yes, I have. I played them at my fifth birthday party.

Unit 5. Tests A and B. Test Booklet. Activity 2. Test A. Listen Then write *T = True* or *F = False.* Test B. Listen. Then write.

W: Hi. I'm Zoe. I love music. Last week I went to two concerts. They were great. In the first concert I heard a girl play the piano. She was ten. I've never heard anyone play the piano that young. Her fingers played so quickly. She played classical music. Then there was a boy who was twelve. He played the cello. Have you ever played the cello? It doesn't look easy.
The second concert was very different. It was a band. There were six men in the band. They played some reggae music and disco. I've never been to such a noisy concert! One man played the harmonica. Two men were playing saxophones. I love the saxophone. I want to play the saxophone one day. Then there was a man on the drums. One man in the band was playing a tambourine and a triangle – but I couldn't see him. And ... the sixth man in the band was singing.

Unit 6

Unit 6. Tests A and B. Test Booklet. Activity 1. Test A. Listen Then write *T = True* or *F = False.* Test B. Listen. Then tick (✓) or cross (✗).

M: What shall we do today, Rachel?

W: Shall we go to the theme park?

M: I'm not sure. What else could we do?

W: We could go to the water park?

M: No ... I don't like water parks. I can't swim! Shall we go to the shopping centre?

W: Er ... no. I don't like shopping.

M: Could we go to the castle?

W: Yes! I love castles.

M: Then we'll go to the museum with mum and dad.

W: Yes. Great idea!

Unit 6. Tests A and B. Test Booklet. Activity 2. Test A. Listen. Then write. Test B. Listen. Then number in the correct order.

M: Hi, Jan. What will you do today at the theme park?

W: Hi, Ben. First I'll go on the big wheel. I love the big wheel. Then, I'll go on the rollercoaster.

M: Will they make you ill?

W: No. I'll be fine. Then I'll go on the boating lake for an hour.

M: What else?

W: Er ... then I'll go on the dodgems and then the pirate ship.

M: Will you play mini-golf?

W: I might do. I'll play mini-golf last – if I've got time!

Unit 7

Unit 7. Tests A and B. Test Booklet. Activity 1. Test A. Listen. Then write *T = True* or *F = False.* Test B. Listen. Then complete.

M: I love looking at the stars. My Dad shows me the different planets. I can't remember all of them. I should draw them in a notebook and write the names next to them. Tonight we're going to look at Mars. My Dad's got a new telescope and he wants to use it. We should see some of the planets that are closer to Earth.
I love reading sci-fi stories, too. I'm reading a story about an alien from Mars. He meets an astronaut in space. The alien goes into the astronaut's rocket, but the rocket isn't very big. The alien has got a spaceship. It's bigger than the rocket. He invites the astronaut to his spaceship. And ...
They travel through space together and see different stars, planets and comets. They have lots of adventures.
Oh ... I'd better get ready. I need to put on some warm clothes because it might be cold outside tonight. My Dad's got the telescope ready. Coming Dad!!'

Unit 7. Tests A and B. Test Booklet. Activity 2. Test A. Listen. Then write. Test B. Listen. Then match.

1

M: Which is the most interesting story you've ever read, Carla?

W: Oh ... that's a difficult question. Harry Potter is the best story ... but most interesting ...

2

M: What has been your most amazing journey?

W: That's easy. The journey by train to China. I went with my family two years ago. It was really amazing.

3

M: Which of your Dad's telescopes is the most expensive?

W: Oh ... He's got so many. His newest telescope is the most complicated so it might be the most expensive, too.

4

M: Which is your worst photo?

W: There's a photograph of me when I was seven. It's horrible. I had really short hair ... ugh!!!

5

M: Which is the most frightening film you have seen?

W: I think 'Space Aliens' is the most frightening film I have seen.

6

M: Which astronaut is the most important?

W: I don't think there is one important astronaut. I think they're all important. The first man to go into space was important ... but I don't think he was more important than the other astronauts.

Unit 8

Unit 8. Tests A and B. Test Booklet. Activity 1. Test A. Listen. Then number in the correct order. Test B. Listen. Then write *T = True* or *F = False.*

W: This week I'm going to help protect the environment.
On Monday, I'm going to go to school on my bike or take the bus.
On Tuesday, I'm going to take the

green and brown bottles to the bottle bank in my town.
On Wednesday, I'm going to collect all the rubbish at school and at home.
On Thursday, I'm going to put paper I don't want in a recycling bin.
On Friday, I'm going to turn off all the lights when I'm the last person to go out of a room.
On Saturday, I'm going to take old plastic bags to use when I go shopping with Mum and Dad.

Unit 8. Tests A and B. Test Booklet. Activity 2. Test A. Listen. Then write *T = True* or *F = False*. Test B. Listen. Then match.

1

M1: What can we do to help protect the environment? Jenny, what can you do?

W1: I can turn off my bedroom light because we need to conserve energy.

2

M1: What can you do, Steve?

M2: I can help keep the planet clean. I can tidy my room and put all the rubbish in a bin.

3

M1: Hilary, what can you do?

W2: I can do lots of things. I can reduce waste by reusing plastic bags.

4

M1: Great. And Tony, what can you do?

M3: I can save resources by putting empty bottles in the recycling bin.

5

M1: And, Ed, what can you do?

M4: I can help save the rainforests by recycling paper.

6

M1: What can you do, Vicky?

W3: I can use public transport to go to school. I usually go by car but next week I can go by bus.

End of term 1

End of term Test 1. Units 1 to 3. Test Booklet. Activity 1. Listen. Then complete.

Wendy

W: I'm eight. I love camping. At the moment, I'm putting in the tent pegs.

After that, I'm lighting a campfire. I love campfires. Tomorrow morning, we're taking down the tents. Then we're hiking fifteen kilometres. We're hiking to a big campsite next to the sea. It's very quiet.

Sebastian

M1: I'm ten. I love hiking, but I don't like sailing. At the moment, I'm on a fishing trip on a river! It's raining and I'm wet and cold. I want to keep out of the rain. We've got a small green tent. I can pitch the tent. Then I'll be warm and dry!

Martin

M2: I'm eleven. I love climbing. I've got a small grey and green rucksack. In my rucksack, I've got a blue sleeping bag, a torch and my climbing shoes. Tomorrow morning, we're climbing a mountain next to the campsite. I'm very excited but a little scared!

End of term Test 1. Units 1 to 3. Test Booklet. Activity 2. Listen. Then write.

1

M1: How heavy is it?

W: It's six hundred and fifty kilograms.

2

M1: How heavy is it?

M2: It's eight hundred and four kilograms.

3

M1: How heavy are they?

W: They're three hundred and thirteen kilograms.

4

M1: How long is it?

M2: It's five metres long.

5

M1: How long are they?

W: They're two and a half metres.

End of term Test 1. Units 1 to 3. Test Booklet. Activity 3. Listen. Then number in the correct order.

1

M: How do I get to the stadium, please?

W: First you go straight ahead and walk to the end of the road.

M: OK.

W: Then you turn left.

M: OK.

W: Then you continue straight until you get to a big guest house.

M: OK.

W: Then you turn right and walk along the road.

M: OK.

W: Then you go past the fire station and turn right at the bus stop.

M: OK.

W: The stadium is directly in front of you.

2

M: How do I get to the bookshop, please?

W: First you go to the end of the road.

M: OK.

W: Then you need to go across the road.

M: Right.

W: Continue walking and when you can see the university, turn right.

M: OK.

W: Then, at the next traffic lights, turn left.

M: OK.

W: Then you continue along this road to the railway station.

M: OK.

W: The bookshop is opposite the station.

M: Thank you.

End of term 2

End of term Test 2. Units 4 to 6. Test Booklet. Activity 1. Listen. Then number in the correct order.

M: Yesterday I made dinner. We had pasta.
I boiled some water and put the pasta in.
I got some tomatoes and cut them in half.
I cooked the tomatoes in olive oil.
Then I put the pasta on a plate.
The plate fell onto the floor.
The plate didn't break but the pasta was all over the floor.
We couldn't have pasta.
So ... I cooked some chicken and rice.

End of term Test 2. Units 4 to 6. Test Booklet. Activity 2. Listen and circle.

W: It was Thursday and Richard was in bed. He was ill. And he was angry. At school, his team were playing football. It was an important game and he was missing it!
His mum took him to the doctor's. When Ellie came home from school, she gave her brother some sweets. Later, Richard's friend Roland brought some books for him to read. Mum made some hot soup and spaghetti but Richard didn't want it. He wasn't hungry.

End of term Test 2. Units 4 to 6. Test Booklet. Activity 3. Listen. Then match.

1

M1: What will you do today, Sue?

W1: First I'll go to the palace and then I'll play mini-golf.

2

M1: What will you do today, Julie?

W2: I'll go to the museum and then go on the pirate ship.

3

M1: What will you do today, Mike?

M2: I'll go to the water park and go on the boating lake. I love the boating lake.

4

M1: What will you do today, Sam?

M3: I'll go to the castle first. Then I'll go on the rollercoaster.

5

M1: What will you do today, Charlotte?

W3: I'll go to the aquarium and then I'll go on the carousel.

6

M1: What will you do today, Brett?

M4: I'll go to the theme park and go on the dodgems.

End of term 3
End of term Test 3. Units 7 and 8. Test Booklet. Activity 1. Listen. Then circle.

M: I'm reading a great book at the moment. It's about an alien. He's really intelligent. The story tells you about his amazing journey through space. He visits lots of different planets and meets some very scary monsters. It's like a frightening sci-fi film!
Then one day a boy wants to look at the night sky. He asks his Dad if he can use his Dad's new telescope. His Dad says yes but it's a very complicated telescope. Dad says he'll help his son to use it.
They look at the sky every night. Then one night, they see a really big star. 'What's that?' the boy asks his Dad. 'I haven't seen that star before.'
A little later, the star moves really quickly and … it lands in their back garden. 'We'd better get ready for aliens.' Dad says to the boy. 'No way!' The boy and his dad go out into the garden and …
I'm not going to tell you the rest … It's a really interesting story and an important lesson. It's all about helping each other and trying to understand each other. You ought to read it!

End of term Test 3. Units 7 and 8. Test Booklet. Activity 2. Listen. Then tick (✓).

W: I'm Debbie. My family and friends are going to help our environment this week. We're going to clean up our park and streets.
My family are going to the park. We're going to collect all the rubbish. We're going to wear plastic gloves to keep our hands clean.
My friend's family usually travel by car. Next week, they're going to use the bus and train.
Mr Brown lives in the house next to mine. He's going to collect paper and recycle it.
And Mrs Noble is going to take all the empty bottles to the bottle bank. It's going to be fun!

End of term Test 3. Units 7 and 8. Test Booklet. Activity 3. Listen. Then complete.

W: We're studying space at school at the moment and have to do a project for our homework. I've chosen to find out about the first woman in space. Her name was Valentina Tereshkova. That's T – E – R – E – S – H – K – O – V – A and she was Russian. She flew in the rocket Vostok 6 that's V – O – S – T – O – K 6. The rocket was launched on June the 16th 1963. That's a very long time ago! She was flying in space for three days and went round Earth 48 times. When she came back to Earth, a lot of journalists wanted to talk to her and write her story.

Final Test
Final Tests A and B. Test Booklet. Activity 1. Test A. Listen. Then circle. Test B. Listen. Then complete.

M: I'm going to the mountains next weekend. I can't wait! I'm going camping with my aunt and uncle. They go every weekend. I'm taking my green and purple rucksack and a compass. I learnt to read a compass last summer.
I'll put my new sleeping bag in the rucksack. My uncle is taking the tent and my aunt is taking the sleeping bags. We're going to make a campfire and cook on the fire. My favourite camp food is rice and beans.

Final Tests A and B. Test Booklet. Activity 2. Test A. Listen. Then tick (✓). Test B. Listen. Then write T = True or F = False.

W1: Hi, Hilary. What wild animals have you seen?

W2: I've seen lots of wild animals.

W1: Have you seen a rhino?

W2: No, I haven't.

W1: Have you seen a camel?

W2: Yes, I have. I saw a camel in Egypt last year.

W1: Have you seen a cheetah?

W2: No, I haven't.

W1: Have you seen a whale?

W2: Yes, I have. I saw a whale in Argentina.

W1: Have you seen a turtle?

W2: Yes, I have. I saw some wild turtles in Greece last summer.

W1: Hi, Pete. What animals have you seen? Have you seen a rhino?

M: Yes, I have. I saw one in the wildlife park.

W1: Have you seen a camel?

M: No, I haven't.

W1: Have you seen a cheetah?

M: No, I haven't.

W1: Have you seen a whale?

M: Yes, I have. I saw a whale last year. It was really big.

W1: Have you seen a turtle?

M: No, I haven't.

Final Tests A and B. Test Booklet. Activity 3. Test A. Listen and complete. Test B. Listen and circle.

1

W1: Engineering is more complicated than History. You need to know Maths.

2

W2: Theme parks are more exciting than computer games, but they can be scary.

3

W1: Music is easier than Geography, and I like the Music teacher more.

4

W2: I want to buy the most complicated telescope, but it's too expensive.

5

W1: Riding a horse is more difficult than riding a bike, and it's more expensive.

6

W2: Reading a book can be more interesting than watching a film, but it takes longer.

7

W1: A house is more expensive than a car, but some cars are very expensive.

Final Tests A and B. Test Booklet. Activity 4. Test A. Listen. Then number. Test B. Listen. Then match.

M: I'm Owen and I'm in a band. There are six people in the band. We're going to have a concert for our families. I'm going to play the drums. Then Stuart, he's going to play the saxophone. He's really good. Then Paul is going to play the triangle. Ben always plays the tambourine. And Michelle is going to play the clarinet. We're going to play instruments and Alice is going to sing.

Exam Preparation Test
Exam preparation. Tests A and B. Test Booklet. Activity 1. Listen and draw lines.

1

W1: Are you going to do a project on the environment at school?

W2: Yes, we are. Everyone in the class is going to do something.

W1: Who's the boy with the two bags?

W2: That's Ben.

W1: What's he going to do?

W2: He's going to collect rubbish from the park and put it in the bin.

2

W1: And, who's the girl next to the bottles? She looks very busy.

W2: Ah yes. That's Jessica. She's really excited about the project.

W1: What's she going to do?

W2: She's going to save resources.

W1: Ah … she's saving resources by recycling bottles?

W2: Yes.

3

W1: And … can you see the boy over there?

W2: Where?

W1: Over there … the boy with the blond hair.

W2: The boy in the kitchen?

W1: Yes. What's his name?

W2: His name is Frank.

W1: What's Frank going to do?

W2: He's going to conserve energy by turning off the lights.

4

W1: So … who's the girl in the shop?

W2: The girl re-using the plastic bag? That's Pam. She's going to reduce waste.

5

W1: OK. Now, there are two more children I don't know. Can you see them?

W2: Fiona is next to the paper recycling bin. She's going to save trees by recycling paper.

6

W1: Ah, yes … and the other boy …

W2: That's Trevor. He's going to help reduce pollution. He usually goes to school by car but now he's going to catch the bus every day.

Exam preparation. Tests A and B. Test Booklet. Activity 2. Test A. Listen. Then write. Test B. Listen. Then correct the mistakes.

W1: I'd like to ask you some questions about your last holiday. Have you got a moment?

W2: Yes.

W1: What's your name?

W2: My name's Samantha.

W1: Samantha. How do you spell that?

W2: S – A – M – A – N – T – H – A.

W1: OK. What class are you in, Samantha?

W2: I'm in class 5T.

W1: 5G?

W2: No, 5 T – T for ten.

W1: Where did you go on holiday?

W2: We went to Argentina.

W1: Who did you go with?

W2: I went with my mum and dad and my sisters.

W1: How many sisters have you got?

W2: I've got two sisters.

W1: What places did you visit?

W2: We visited a wildlife park and a theme park.

W1: What animals did you see in the wildlife park?

W2: We saw lots of different animals.

W1: Did you see any camels?

W2: No, we didn't see any camels.

W1: Did you see any giraffes?

W2: Yes, we saw one giraffe. It was very tall.

W1: What else did you see?

W2: We saw some tigers and I think I saw a lemur.

W1: A lemur? Are you sure?!

W2: I think so – but no one else saw it.

W1: OK. And … what was your favourite activity?

W2: My favourite activity … er …

W1: What about the wildlife park?

W2: No … I liked that but my favourite activity was going to the theme park. That was amazing!

Exam preparation. Tests A and B. Test Booklet. Activity 3. What are the children going to take on their camping holiday? Listen and draw lines.

1

W1: Hi, Chris. Are you going on the school camping holiday?

M1: Yes, I am. Are you?

W1: Yes. I'm really excited. What are you going to take?

M1: I'm going to take a map and a compass. I love map reading and I'm going to help the teachers find the route.

2

M2: What are you going to take, Joanna?

W1: I'm going to take a torch.

M2: Good idea. You can see better at night with a torch!

W1: Yes.

3

W1: Are you going on the camping holiday, Martin?

M3: Yes, I am. I love camping.

W1: What are you going to take?

M3: I'm going to take a tent. It's a big tent and it's going to be heavy. Two friends are going to help me.

4

W1: Are you going to help Martin carry the tent, Annabel?

W2: Yes, I am. I'm going to take the tent pegs and a sleeping bag.

W1: It's going to be great fun. I can't wait!

Exam preparation. Tests A and B. Test Booklet. Activity 4. Listen. Then tick (✓) the box.

1

M: Did you enjoy your visit to the wildlife park, Zoe?

W1: Yes. I had a great time.

M: What animals did you see?

W1: I saw some lions and some elephants. I saw lots of monkeys; they were everywhere!

M: Did you see any rhinos?

W1: Yes, I saw one rhino. I didn't see any snakes or insects.

M: You were lucky!

2

W1: What did you do last week, Vicky?

W2: I did a project at school.

W1: What was the project?

W2: Helping protect our environment.

W1: What did you do to help the environment?

W2: I wanted to help conserve energy.

W1: That's great. How did you do that?

W2: I checked all the lights were turned off in the house if there wasn't anyone in the room.

W1: Were a lot of lights on?

W2: Yes, there were.

3

W1: Hi, Fiona. What are you doing?

W2: Oh ... I'm going into town.

W1: Are you going to the shopping centre?

W2: No ... I'm not.

W1: Oh. I need some food.

W2: No, sorry. I need to get some books for a project I'm doing at school. I'm going to the new bookshop that has just opened in the High Street. Have you been there?

W1: No, I haven't.

W2: I've got to get an atlas and some books on protecting our wildlife. Can I get you anything?

W1: No. No, thank you. See you later.

Exam preparation. Tests A and B. Test Booklet. Activity 5. Listen. Then colour and write.

1

M: Would you like to colour this picture?

W: OK. Shall I colour the alien with the telescope?

M: Yes, all right. Colour the telescope red and brown.

W: OK!

2

M: Now can you colour two of the stars?

W: Which stars? Shall I colour the biggest stars?

M: No. Colour the two stars closest to the big planet.

W: Oh yes. Can I colour them purple and blue?

M: Yes, OK.

3

M: I'd like you to write something now. Can you see the astronaut in the middle?

W: Yes. He's stretching his arms in front of him.

M: Yes. There's an alien next to him. Can you see it?

W: Yes ... He's got a pen in his hand.

M: Yes. That's the one. I want you to write 'Welcome to Space' next to the astronaut.

W: That's W – E – L – C – O – M – E   T – O   S – P – A – C – E.

M: Yes. That's right.

4

W: Can I colour something now?

M: Yes, of course. Can you colour the boy's spacesuit yellow and orange?

W: OK.

M: Yes. That's fine.

5

M: Now, can you see the alien in the front?

W: The one sitting down pressing the buttons?

M: Yes.

W: OK. Can I colour his spacesuit pink and green?

M: Yes, that's fine.

PUPIL'S NAME	EVALUATION CHART								
	Placement	1	2	3	4	5	6	7	8

MARKING CRITERIA: ★ = Still developing   ★★ = Progressing well   ★★★ = Excellent

Evaluation chart

PUPIL'S NAME	EVALUATION CHART				
	End of term 1	End of term 2	End of term 3	Final	Exam preparation

MARKING CRITERIA: ★ = Still developing   ★★ = Progressing well   ★★★ = Excellent